THE MODERN KOSHER KITCHEN

Fair Winds Press
100 Cummings Center, Suite 406L
Beverly, MA 01915

fairwindspress.com • quarryspoon.com

THE MODERN KOSHER KITCHEN

More than 125 Inspired Recipes *for* a New Generation of Kosher Cooks

Ronnie Fein

First published in the USA in 2015 by
Fair Winds Press, a member of
Quayside Publishing Group
100 Cummings Center
Suite 406-L
Beverly, MA 01915-6101
www.fairwindspress.com
Visit www.QuarrySPOON.com and help us celebrate food
and culture one spoonful at a time!
Visit www.bodymindbeautyhealth.com. It's your personal
guide to a happy, healthy, and extraordinary life!

18 17 16 15 14   1 2 3 4 5

ISBN: 978-1-59233-635-7

Digital edition published in 2015
eISBN: 978-162788-179-1

Library of Congress Cataloging-in-Publication Data available

Design: John Foster at badpeoplegoodthings.com
Photography by Glenn Scott Photography

Printed and bound in China

The information in this book is for educational purposes only.
It is not intended to replace the advice of a physician or medical
practitioner. Please see your health care provider before beginning
any new health program.

For Zev, Lila, Nina, Remy, and Carina,
the next generation of creators.

FOREWORD

RONNIE AND I FIRST MET ALMOST 4 YEARS AGO AT KOSHERFEST, an industry trade show in Secaucus, New Jersey. I was there signing copies of my *Quick & Kosher* cookbook series. She introduced herself with a beaming smile, shining eyes, and an outstretched arm (her other arm wrapped around her new book, *Hip Kosher*). We hugged immediately—both big fans of the other—meeting for the first time.

I loved Ronnie right away; in that initial embrace and during our first exchange I felt like we were old friends. To Ronnie, really, we are one big family, meant to sit together around one big table. Her warmth comes across in her food just as her love of family in her writing.

We spent the next several years getting to know each other through our recipes and words. She began writing regularly for my website, www.joyofkosher.com, delighting us all with her kitchen creativity and quick wit. So I know her work, I know her recipes, and I know that Ronnie knows good food. And good food is what she offers in this wonderful new kosher cookbook chock-full of fabulous, creative, and interesting recipes.

When she first shared the wonderful news that she was writing a new book, I couldn't wait to see what the pages would bring. The modern American kosher kitchen concept was captivating. The recipes in this book seem like recipes from everywhere, and that's what makes them so appealing. At the heart of it, Ronnie understands that kosher cuisine is not limited to the traditional Ashkenazi or Sephardic dishes that most Americans are familiar with. And although Israeli cuisine is enjoying an immensely popular moment, there is an entire world of kosher fare out there. Jewish people have been scattered throughout time, throughout the world, and their cooking has always reflected the cuisine of their neighbors—the kosher version of that cuisine.

Russian home cooks prepared borscht, and Moroccan home cooks prepared chicken tagine; their kosher neighbors cooked the same dishes using kosher ingredients, leaving out any *treif*. This devotion to the laws of *kashruth* is what has held Jews together as a spiritual community, no matter where we lived and no matter what we cooked.

Ronnie has done the same thing for the American community. She has pursued that same sensibility and devotion in her quest to create great-tasting *kosher American* cuisine. Her recipes reflect the way Americans eat in the twenty-first century.

What does that mean? What makes food American?

America is a multicultural mix of people and cuisines. Look at any restaurant menu. Watch a cooking competition. Read Ronnie's blog at www.ronniefein.com. You'll see that when people talk about American food, they mean a big mixture of traditions and flavors from Asian stir-fries to South-western-style barbecued chicken to seasonings such as ras el hanout or dukkah, which are popular in northern Africa and the Middle East.

Ronnie includes all of it here with exotic and fascinating recipes such as Fish Curry with Star Anise, Chile Pepper, and Coconut Milk; Naan Vegetable Pizzas; and Roasted Chicken with Baharat, Garlic, and Mint.

I didn't grow up keeping kosher. In fact, I think it helps that I have an understanding of non-kosher food because I know what great food is supposed to taste like. And I know that kosher food can be equally delicious and perhaps even better than any other cuisine on earth. As a bride who knew nothing about cooking and now a devotee to fast, fresh family food, Ronnie's recipes speak to me. This book makes me want to cook. The enormous variety of recipes will speak to experi-enced home cooks, but novice cooks need not worry. They won't be intimidated by any of the recipes. Ronnie has a very friendly writing style and gives clear in-structions. In addition, there are oodles of tips and helpful hints in many of the recipe sidebars.

Ronnie always describes herself as an "old-timer in the food biz." I think that's funny because her food is so fresh and fabulous, so clever and creative, so acces-sible and attainable. This is a book for anyone who wants to get out of that same-old what-should-we-have-for dinner rut. Exprienced cooks, heads of busy households (like me), newly marrieds, singles, anyone who yearns for something delicious to eat and that's also kosher—although you don't have to be kosher to enjoy these recipes—will find lots to love about *The Modern Kosher Kitchen*.

Love what you did here, Ronnie!

Love,

Jamie Geller

Jamie Geller, author of *Joy of Kosher: Fast, Fresh Family Recipes,* founder of Kosher Media Network, publisher of *Joy of Kosher with Jamie Geller* magazine and www.joyofkosher.com

INTRODUCTION

THE SURGE IN KOSHER COOKING
···

KEEPING KOSHER ISN'T EASY. There are lots of rules to follow, labels to look at, different plates and utensils for different foods. It's a real commitment. So why is it that more and more people are turning to the Jewish dietary laws?

As you would expect, for many people it's about religious observance. Their families have always followed *kashruth*, the laws laid out in the Old Testament books of Leviticus and Deuteronomy (plus various decrees handed down through the centuries by rabbis and other authorities). For Jews who haven't been observant, it is like a return. They feel more committed than their parents were or they feel a spiritual need to follow *kashruth* for what it teaches us beyond the biblical rules: to be mindful of what we eat, to protect the earth and sustain its produce, and to raise animals in a humane environment.

But there is also a broad and growing demographic of people who benefit from *kashruth* for a reason that has nothing to do with religion. It's this: the butchering and labeling requirements for kosher food make it incredibly easy to eat more healthfully, to avoid certain ingredients, and to be sure meat and poultry have been slaughtered properly and are fit to eat.

For an animal to be designated kosher, it must be slaughtered by a *shochet*, who uses special tools that cause the animal to die instantaneously and with minimal pain. The *shochet* then inspects the animal to be sure there are no abnormalities or imperfections that would make the meat unsuitable. To be certified kosher, all packaged products must indicate whether they contain any meat or dairy ingredients; products with neither meat nor dairy are labeled "parve."

All of these stringent requirements mean that those who are concerned about the humane treatment of animals can be confident about buying kosher meat and poultry. And those who are lactose-intolerant, vegetarian, vegan, or allergic to specific ingredients can easily determine whether a product is safe or appropriate for them.

IS KOSHER FOOD THE SAME AS JEWISH FOOD?

Because the majority of Jewish families in the United States are *Ashkenazi*, people who trace their ethnic roots to Central and Eastern Europe, we tend to regard "Jewish" and "kosher" cuisine as a monolith, with the specialties that our *Ashkenazi* grandmas and great-grandmas cooked: stuffed cabbage, blintzes, borscht, and kugel, and with ingredients such as chicken fat *schmaltz* and sour cream that were staples in the *Ashkenazi* kosher kitchen.

These foods are culinary treasures. They're comforting and taste familiar and wonderful as they conjure up memories of holidays with family and loved ones who are no longer with us. But that's not the stuff of our daily dinners anymore. Some of these dishes took all day to prepare, but no one has that kind of time now. Besides, traditional *Ashkenazi* cuisine was loaded with fat, cholesterol, and salt. Artery-cloggers. High blood-pressure-pumpers. Today we know we have to eat smarter and healthier.

And so modern kosher cooks will do what all those who have come before them have done: conform *kashruth* to how we wish to eat now with healthier recipes and dishes that are exciting and use fresh herbs and spices, whole grains, and less meat. Dishes that take advantage of the bounty of produce and products available today. Dishes that Grandma never cooked, using ingredients she never knew existed.

No matter what our backgrounds, many of us are generations away from our immigrant ancestors. Whether we have always been kosher or are new to it, whether or not we are even Jewish, all of us are exposed to modern American cooking when we go out to a restaurant and have a chance to taste what's new and different. We read about food trends, about what's hot. The media constantly alert us to new products, cooking ideas, and imaginative recipes.

Kosher cooking is changing along with these trends. Today more and more of us are cooking with and eating new ingredients. Sriracha-infused mayonnaise. Crème fraiche. Lemongrass, freekeh, ponzu sauce. It gets easier to do all the time, too, because every year thousands of new kosher-certified products become available to meet the demands of sophisticated kosher home cooks.

PANTRY INGREDIENTS

Apple cider vinegar

Fresh fruit: oranges,
  limes, lemons, pears

Chile peppers

Scallions

Tahini

Matzo farfel

Broth: vegetable
  and beef

Sriracha

Spices: cinnamon stick,
  nutmeg, star anise,
  whole cloves, and
  coriander

Fresh ginger

Fresh cilantro

Whole garlic

Red onion

Honey

Coconut milk

Variety of whole grains

Shallots

Variety of beans

I BELIEVE THAT WE CAN NO LONGER DEFINE "JEWISH FOOD." But we can define kosher food, which is *any* kind of food prepared in accordance with the laws of *kashruth*. In America, in the twenty-first century, that means the recipes could be a classic, such as matzo ball soup, or as innovative and non-*Ashkenazi* as farro pilaf with squash, edamame, and pumpkin seeds or fish curry with star anise, chile pepper, and coconut milk.

I wrote this book to try to inspire all home cooks who keep kosher and would like to prepare the kind of foods that informed, sophisticated—hip—folks want to cook today. The recipes I've developed for this book are in keeping with my first kosher cookbook, *Hip Kosher*, and focus on modern American recipes—that is, recipes that are multicultural, innovative, and interesting. I believe these are the kinds of recipes that appeal to the fast-growing audience of kosher home cooks who want to extend their culinary repertoire beyond the more familiar Eastern European or Sephardic traditions, even in their more "modernized versions." As with *Hip Kosher*, recipe selections are globally influenced and the ingredients are all certified kosher and readily available in the American market.

Hip Kosher focused on recipes that could be cooked within 30 minutes, concentrating on family meals while including a smattering of company dishes. The recipes in this book are still fairly easy and quick to cook, but also include some slow-cooked dishes. I've also added highly demanded categories not covered in *Hip Kosher* and requested by my readers: appetizers, breakfast and brunch foods, vegetarian and budget-minded dishes, and Passover recipes. The recipes are innovative and interesting but never intimidating. They have eye appeal but you don't need special talent or professional equipment to cook them.

Each recipe is marked to denote whether it includes dairy or meat or is parve (dairy- and meat-free), but with simple substitutions, some of them can switch from one category to another. Look for sidebars to help here, plus tips about ingredients, equipment, or cooking methods that might make cooking the recipes even easier.

IN THE CABINET AND FRIDGE

If you have a well-stocked kitchen, you'll never be at a loss when you have to cook a meal. I don't mean to say that you need every so-called must-have utensil or every trendy spice blend or condiment. I am talking about the basics, the stuff every home cook should have on hand all the time, plus a few extra items that can make what you cook tastier and more interesting and exciting.

Fortunately for kosher home cooks, thousands of *hekhshered* products (approved kosher by a special certifying agency) are available to help you do just that. Many of these ingredients, which our mothers and certainly our grandmothers never heard of, can move your meals from ordinary to memorable, from old hat to new and exciting, so your family won't say, "This again?" but, "Wow, I love this!"

Surely, you'll want on hand familiar items such as eggs, flour, sugar, salt, black peppercorns, onions, bread crumbs, butter, olive oil, ketchup, and so on. (Note that my recipes assume you'll be using large eggs and unsalted butter.) But also consider the list that follows, which includes some of the foods I always have in my cupboard or fridge. These are the ingredients that add dimension and flexibility to a recipe and help make daily dinners a little less humdrum.

PRODUCE
- Lemons, limes, scallions, parsley, ginger root, and onions (for all-purpose cooking)
- A whole head of garlic (Don't buy the minced garlic in a jar because once you cut garlic, it loses its flavor and tastes rancid.)
- Fresh thyme, rosemary, mint, and basil (Even though dried herbs are handy—I have lots of them—the dried versions of these particular herbs lack the garden flavor and complexity of the fresh kind.)
- Fresh chile peppers (a lively addition to dishes from sauces to soups to stir-fries)

Room for more? Add fresh cilantro and lemongrass.

DAIRY AND NONDAIRY REFRIGERATOR ITEMS
- Cheese such as Parmesan, feta, and goat (for salads, pasta, omelets, and hundreds of other dishes)
- Plain yogurt (preferably Greek style, nonfat)
- Butter (My recipes use unsalted butter, which tastes fresher and cuts down on unnecessary sodium.)
- Margarine (Except on Passover, I always use Earth Balance Buttery Spread, a parve, vegan, healthy, and tasty butter

substitute that is available in sticks and tubs.)
- Milk substitutes: coconut and soy milks (These work admirably in place of dairy in a variety of foods.)

Room for more? I always have kefir in the fridge for smoothies, soups, quick breads, and sauce. Also, tofu and almond milk.

SEASONINGS
- Condiments: Harissa and/or s'chug, Dijon mustard, sriracha, Tabasco sauce, hoisin sauce, sesame oil, mayonnaise, soy sauce, mango chutney, balsamic vinegar, fish sauce (These are used to enhance flavor in a recipe or complement another item in the meal. As of this writing, no authentic anchovy-based fish sauce is available, but Queen of Tuna produces a tuna-based version.)
- Dried herbs and spices: cayenne pepper, chili powder, ground cumin, curry powder, oregano, paprika, crushed red pepper, wasabi powder, ground cinnamon, ground ginger, whole nutmegs (plus a nutmeg grater), whole cloves (All are used often and for numerous recipes and categories of food.)
- Pure vanilla extract (It costs more than imitation vanilla but is well worth it for its fragrance and flavor.)

Room for more? Think Sambal (another type of chili mixture used to give heat and complexity to foods), Aleppo pepper, ground coriander, and spice blends such as ras el hanout and za'atar.

ALL-PURPOSE CUPBOARD ITEMS
- Canned beans (white, black, and chickpeas) and packaged lentils
- Stock: vegetable, beef, and chicken
- Whole grains: rice, brown rice, freekeh, farro, quinoa
- Sweeteners: honey, maple syrup
- Chocolate: unsweetened and semi-sweet or bittersweet
- Pasta: spaghetti, rice noodles
- Canned tomatoes
- Vinegar: red and white wine vinegars, apple cider vinegar
- Canned coconut milk
- Panko
- Tomato paste
- Dried fruit: cranberries, raisins, apricots

Room for more? Look at oat groats, spelt, and wheat berries, gluten-free corn pasta, mirin, rice vinegar, chipotles in adobo (hot and smoky chile peppers that boost flavor in soups, sauces, and sandwiches).

FREEZER ITEMS

- Frozen peas, corn, edamame, and spinach (for tons of recipes from salads to soups to casseroles)
- Puff pastry (for tarts and casseroles)
- Poultry and meat bones (for soups, stews, and homemade tomato sauce)
- Pizza dough (for a quick meal)
- Fresh cranberries (You might want to cook them in the summer!)
- Nuts (For longer storage and fresher taste, keep them frozen in plastic bags or containers.)

SPECIALTY ITEMS

- Facon, from Jack's Gourmet (To paraphrase Shakespeare, "How do I love thee? Let me count the ways!" This beef bacon is smoky, salty, and well seasoned; a sensation, the best, tastiest version of faux treif I've ever tasted. I've used it for every part of a meat meal, but especially love the BLTs with Arugula and Basil-Mayo, page 19. Jack's also has chorizo and other types of sausages.) Go to www.jacksgourmetkosher.com.

- Grow and Behold "lamb-type" Merguez sausage (It's lamby but not gamey. It's popular in North Africa with couscous, but I use it for all sorts of dishes, including the Merguez Shakshuka, page 138.) Go to www.growandbehold.com.
- KOL Foods kielbasa (It's tasty on the grill. As is.) Go to www.kolfoods.com.

RECIPE ICONS

 Recipe contains dairy

 Recipe contains meat

 Recipe is parve (does not contain meat or dairy)

APPETIZERS

When people entertain they usually have some idea about what to cook for dinner, but to figure out what to serve for starters always seems a lot harder. Appetizers give guests their first impression of what's to come, so the choices should be not only tasty but also welcoming and visually appealing. Yet, how many of us have the time to fuss with elaborate tidbits in addition to a meal? This chapter will help. It includes recipes for a variety of appetizers, most of which can be made ahead. All are attractive but not intimidating or too complicated to prepare.

BLTS WITH ARUGULA
AND BASIL-MAYO

(M)

Thanks to excellent beef bacon, kosher cooks can feast on BLTs.
These are mini and seasoned with basil and arugula, which give
a fresh garden flavor to the classic sandwich.

4 ounces (115 g) beef bacon

8 slices home-style white bread

1/2 cup (115 g) mayonnaise

2 tablespoons (5 g) finely
chopped fresh basil

8 thin slices tomato

1/4 cup (5 g) chopped arugula

Fancy toothpicks

Cook the bacon in a sauté pan over medium heat for 4 to 5 minutes, turning the pieces occasionally, or until crispy. Remove the bacon from the pan and drain on paper towels. Lightly toast the bread slices. Trim the crusts from the bread.

Mix the mayonnaise and basil and spread equal amounts on each slice of toast. Crumble the bacon evenly over each of four of the toast slices. Cover each with the tomato slices. Scatter the arugula evenly over the tomatoes. Top each with the remaining toast slices.

Cut each sandwich into 3 equal portions lengthwise, then 3 or 4 slices widthwise. Skewer each mini sandwich with a fancy toothpick.

Yield: Makes 36 to 48 mini sandwiches

SERVING SUGGESTIONS AND SUBSTITUTIONS: It's simple to make this into a parve dish by eliminating the bacon. Use a layer of thinly sliced avocado or hard-cooked egg instead. Yes, the sandwiches taste entirely different but get plenty of flavor from the fresh arugula and basil.

POTATO CAKES

You can never have enough of these. These potato cakes are crispy, salty, spicy, and ultra-satisfying. They freeze well, too, and, I have to say, I have seen members of my family eat these straight from the freezer.

For the Filling:

1½ pounds (680 g) all-purpose potatoes

2 tablespoons (30 ml) vegetable oil

1 medium onion, chopped

3 tablespoons (3 g) chopped fresh cilantro

1½ teaspoons (3 g) chopped fresh ginger

1 teaspoon (2 g) ground coriander

1 teaspoon (2.5 g) ground cumin

¼ teaspoon cayenne pepper, optional

1 tablespoon (15 ml) lemon juice

Salt and freshly ground black pepper, to taste

For the Dough:

3 cups (375 g) all-purpose flour

1 cup (235 ml) boiling water

⅓ cup (80 ml) cold water

Vegetable oil

TIP

I make these when I have time, cut them into wedges, and store them in plastic bags in the freezer. To reheat, place the wedges in a single layer on a cookie sheet in a preheated 425°F (220°C, or gas mark 7) oven for a couple of minutes per side.

Make the Filling: Peel the potatoes, cut them into chunks, and cook in lightly salted water for about 15 minutes or until tender. Drain, mash, and set aside. Heat the vegetable oil in a sauté pan over medium heat and cook the onion for about 3 minutes or until it has softened. Add to the potatoes. Add the cilantro, ginger, coriander, cumin, cayenne, if using, lemon juice, salt, and pepper, and mash the ingredients until smooth and evenly distributed. Let cool.

Make the Dough: Place the flour in the bowl of an electric mixer or food processor. Add the boiling water and mix at medium speed (or process) until a rough dough has formed. Let cool for 2 to 3 minutes. Pour in the cold water and mix or process for 3 to 4 minutes until the dough forms into a smooth ball. Remove and divide the dough into 6 pieces. Using a rolling pin on a lightly floured surface, roll 1 piece of dough at a time into a 10-inch (25-cm) circle. Brush with 1 1/2 teaspoons vegetable oil.

Place about 6 tablespoons (84 g) of the potato filling on top and spread with a knife evenly over the surface, leaving a small rim around the edge. Roll the circles jelly-roll style. Form each rolled dough into a coil. Press down on the coil to flatten it slightly. Gently roll each coil into a circle about 9 to 10 inches (23 to 25 cm) in diameter. Keep the circles separated.

Heat a small amount of vegetable oil in a skillet large enough to hold the circles. Cover the pan and cook each circle, one at a time, over medium-high heat for about 2 minutes per side, or until browned and crispy. Add more vegetable oil to the pan as necessary for each circle of dough. Drain the fried circles on paper towels. Cut each circle into 8 to 12 wedges. Serve hot.

Yield: Makes 48 to 72 pieces

MANGO SHOOTERS

(D)

I love using kefir for muffins, quick breads, smoothies, and cold soups. This recipe started out as soup but then I realized it would be useful for appetizers also, to make adorable drinks served in shot glasses.

2 large mangos

1⅓ cups (315 ml) plain kefir

⅔ cup (160 ml) milk

1 to 1½ teaspoons (3 to 4.5 g) chopped chile pepper

2 tablespoons (40 g) honey

1½ tablespoons (9 g) chopped fresh mint

4 teaspoons (20 ml) lime juice

Nutmeg, grated

Peel the mangos and cut the flesh into chunks. Place the mango, kefir, milk, chile pepper, honey, mint, and lime juice in a blender (or use a deep vessel and hand blender) and purée the ingredients. Pour into shot glasses. Serve at room temperature or slightly chilled. Garnish with a few sprinkles of freshly grated nutmeg.

Yield: Makes about 2 dozen shooters

SERVING SUGGESTIONS AND VARIATIONS: Add salt and serve this mixture as a first-course cold soup!

SMOKED SALMON TARTAR ROUNDS WITH HORSERADISH CREAM CHEESE Ⓓ

These tidbits are so elegant and pretty they look as if you've fussed. But they are incredibly easy to put together. Don't think you have to buy expensive hand-sliced salmon: Many stores sell the much cheaper ends and scraps from that hand-cut salmon, and you'll be chopping the fish anyway, so why not take advantage?

1/2 pound (225 g) smoked salmon

1 thick scallion, finely chopped

1 tablespoon (9 g) chopped capers

2 tablespoons (8 g) chopped fresh dill

1 tablespoon (15 ml) olive oil

1 teaspoon (5 ml) lemon juice

Freshly ground black pepper, to taste

6 tablespoons (90 g) cream cheese, softened

1 1/2 teaspoons (7.5 g) prepared white horseradish

Melba rounds or toasted white bread (cut into rounds)

Grape tomatoes, sliced and cut in half crosswise, optional

Place the salmon on a chopping board and cut into shreds, then turn the shreds and chop them into dice. Add the scallion, capers, and dill and continue to chop until the ingredients are finely minced and evenly distributed. Transfer to a bowl, pour in the olive oil and lemon juice, and stir into the salmon mixture. Season with black pepper to taste. Set aside.

In a small bowl, combine the cream cheese and horseradish. Spread equal amounts of the cream cheese mixture onto the Melba rounds. Spoon equal amounts of the salmon mixture on top. Garnish the tops with a half slice of grape tomato, if desired.

Yield: Makes 24 to 30 pieces

SERVING SUGGESTIONS AND VARIATIONS: Make this into a parve dish by leaving out the cheese; serve the salmon tartar as is on the Melba rounds (or use zucchini slices). If you like, add a tiny dab of mayo mixed with lemon peel on top as a garnish.

SEARED TUNA STEAK STICKS WITH WASABI-SESAME DIP

(P)

This dish is perfect for parties because so much of the prep work can be done ahead of time.

For the Tuna Sticks:

1/3 cup (80 ml) soy sauce

1/4 cup (60 ml) orange juice

1 tablespoon (15 ml) vegetable oil

2 teaspoons (10 ml) sesame seed oil

3 scallions, chopped

1 tablespoon (6 g) chopped fresh ginger

1 pound (455 g) tuna

Vegetable oil, for the pan

For the Wasabi-Sesame Dip:

1 tablespoon (6 g) wasabi powder

1 tablespoon (15 ml) water

1/2 cup (115 g) mayonnaise

1 clove garlic, finely chopped

2 to 3 teaspoons (10 to 15 ml) rice vinegar

Few drops sesame oil

Make the Tuna Sticks: Combine the soy sauce, orange juice, vegetable oil, sesame seed oil, scallions, and ginger in a medium bowl. Cut the tuna into 1-inch (2.5-cm) chunks. Place the tuna chunks in the soy sauce mixture, toss to coat all the pieces, and let marinate for at least 2 to 3 hours.

Heat a film of vegetable oil in a sauté pan over medium-high heat. Add the tuna chunks a few pieces at a time and sear all sides until all the surfaces of the fish are crispy brown. Skewer each cube with a fancy toothpick and serve with the Wasabi-Sesame Dip.

Make the Wasabi-Sesame Dip: Make the wasabi paste by mixing the wasabi powder with the water. Add the mayonnaise, garlic, rice vinegar, and sesame oil. Mix and let rest for about 15 minutes before serving. Makes 1/2 cup (120 g).

Yield: Makes about 21/2 dozen tuna sticks

SERVING SUGGESTIONS AND VARIATIONS: You can make this into dinner: Use a slightly larger amount of tuna (6 ounces, or 170 g, per person) and pan sear or grill the pieces of fish without cutting them into small chunks. Alternatively, slice the cooked tuna steaks, add some tomato slices, and make it into a sandwich, using the dip to slather the bread.

ROASTED POTATO SKINS

(D)

You know that parlor game where people ask, "if you could only have one food what would it be?" My answer is always "baked potato," and, more specifically, "baked potato skins" because the crunch is almost exhilarating, the mineral-y flavor beyond delectable. Add cheese, fresh rosemary, and those tangy little flakes or crystals of sea salt and you've got a winning formula. Cut them into small pieces for the perfect appetizer.

Yogurt Dip, optional
(see sidebar for recipe)

4 large baking potatoes
(Idaho or russet)

2 tablespoons (30 ml) olive oil

2 tablespoons (3.5 g) chopped
fresh rosemary

Sea salt and freshly ground black
pepper, to taste

1 cup (115 g) finely shredded
Monterey Jack cheese

TIP

It's important to use russet or Idaho potatoes because they have thick skins that hold up well in the oven heat.

Yogurt Dip:

1½ cups (345 g) plain yogurt

3 scallions, chopped

Lemon juice, about 1 teaspoon

Mix the yogurt, scallions, and lemon juice. Serve with the Potato Skins, if desired.

Yield: Makes 1½ cups (370 g)

Make the Yogurt Dip, if desired. Set aside. Preheat the oven to 400°F (200°C, or gas mark 6). Scrub the potatoes, pierce them with the tines of a fork, and roast them for about 1 hour or until tender. Remove the potatoes from the oven. Raise the oven heat to 450°F (230°C, or gas mark 8). When the potatoes are cool enough to handle, cut them in half lengthwise and scoop out most of the flesh, leaving a thin layer attached to the skin. Cut the skins crosswise (about 40 pieces). Brush both sides of each piece with the olive oil. Place the skins on a cookie sheet, inside up. Sprinkle with rosemary, a few grindings of sea salt, and pepper. Roast for 5 minutes. Turn the skins over; roast for 5 minutes. Turn the skins inside up again and roast for 5 minutes. Sprinkle the pieces with the cheese. Roast for 3 or 4 minutes or until the cheese has melted and is bubbly. Serve plain or with the yogurt dip.

Yield: Makes 40 pieces

SPICY LAMB PUFFS

(M)

These freeze well so you can make them in advance and pop them into the oven when needed.

2 tablespoons (30 ml) vegetable oil

1 medium onion, chopped

1 teaspoon chopped fresh ginger

12 ounces (340 g) ground lamb

2 teaspoons chopped fresh mint

1/4 teaspoon ground cinnamon

2 pinches grated nutmeg

Salt and freshly ground black pepper, to taste

1 tablespoon (8 g) all-purpose flour

1/4 cup (60 ml) vegetable or beef stock

1/4 cup (28 g) dried currants

2 tablespoons (18 g) crushed pistachios or pine nuts

8 squares frozen parve puff pastry

Egg wash (1 egg beaten with 1 teaspoon water)

Heat the vegetable oil in a sauté pan over medium heat. Add the onion and ginger and cook, stirring occasionally, for about 3 minutes or until the onion has softened. Add the lamb, mint, cinnamon, nutmeg, salt, and pepper. Cook, stirring occasionally and breaking up the meat, for about 3 minutes or until the meat is completely brown. Sprinkle in the flour and mix it in. Pour in the stock and cook until the mixture has thickened. Remove the pan from the heat, mix in the currants and nuts, and set aside to cool.

Thaw the puff pastry. On a lightly floured surface and working with one square at a time, roll each square into a larger 6-inch (15-cm) square. Cut the square into 4 smaller squares. Place about 1 tablespoon (15 g) of the cooled lamb filling in the center of each square. Rub some of the egg wash on two sides of each square, then fold the dough over to form a triangle, pressing down on the sides to seal the filling. Brush the surface with some egg wash. Pierce the surface with the tines of a fork. Refrigerate for at least 15 minutes.

Preheat the oven to 375°F (190°C, or gas mark 5). Bake on ungreased cookie sheets for about 15 minutes or until golden brown.

Yield: Makes 32 puffs

NAAN VEGETABLE PIZZAS

(D)

Pizza has come a long way from the classic Margherita! Almost anything goes now for both crust and toppings. This version is made with naan, a soft, chewy East Indian flatbread that becomes lightly crispy when you bake it, not crunchy like standard pizza dough. The topping is loaded with cauliflower and carrots as well as cheese, so it's a good way to serve some extra vegetables to the naysayers.

2 cups (200 g) cauliflower broken
into very small pieces

1½ (22.5 ml) tablespoons olive oil

Salt and freshly ground black pepper, to taste

1 teaspoon curry powder

2 naan breads

½ cup (125 g) mango chutney

2 cooked carrots, chopped

½ cup (60 g) shredded mozzarella cheese

¼ cup (38 g) grated Gouda cheese

TIP

If the mango chutney has large chunks of fruit, chop them slightly to make the appetizers easier to eat.

Preheat the oven to 400°F (200°C, or gas mark 6). Lightly grease a large cookie sheet or line it with parchment paper. Place the cauliflower pieces on the cookie sheet, pour the olive oil on top and toss the pieces to coat them. Sprinkle with the salt, pepper, and curry powder. Roast for about 20 minutes, turning the vegetables once or twice, or until the cauliflower is softened and just beginning to brown. Remove the cauliflower from the cookie sheet and set aside in a bowl. Place both naan breads on the cookie sheet. Spread equal amounts of the chutney on each bread. Scatter the cauli-flower and carrots on top. Scatter the mozzarella and Gouda cheeses over the vegetables. Bake for about 15 minutes or until the vegetables are hot, the cheese has melted, and the pizzas look toasty. Cut into pieces and serve.

Yield: Makes about 16 to 18 pieces

SERVING SUGGESTIONS AND VARIATIONS: If you can't find naan, use pita bread.

VIDALIA ONION FRITTERS WITH SAMBAL-YOGURT DIP

(D)

Although fried food can become soggy if you don't eat it right away, you can reheat these to crispiness in a hot oven (400°F [200°C, or gas mark 6]) for about 4 minutes per side. Make them larger and they're a good side dish, especially for grilled fish.

For the Yogurt Dip:

1/2 cup (115 g) plain Greek style yogurt

1 garlic clove, finely chopped

1 tablespoon (15 ml) lemon juice

1/2 to 1 teaspoon sambal or sriracha

1/2 teaspoon freshly grated lemon peel

Salt, to taste

For the Fritters:

1 cup (125 g) all-purpose flour

1 teaspoon baking powder

1/2 teaspoon salt, or to taste

3/4 cup (175 ml) milk

1 large egg

1/2 teaspoon sambal

2 medium Vidalia onions, chopped

Vegetable oil, for deep-frying

Make the Yogurt Dip: Place the yogurt, garlic, lemon juice, sambal, lemon peel, and salt in a bowl and mix to blend ingredients thoroughly. Makes 1/2 cup (133 g).

Make the Fritters: Preheat the oven to 200°F (100°C). Place the flour, baking powder, and salt in a large bowl and mix to combine ingredients. Beat the milk, egg, and sambal together. Add the egg mixture and onions to the flour mixture and mix to blend ingredients.

Heat 1/2 inch (1.3 cm) vegetable oil in a deep sauté pan. When the oil is hot enough for a crumb of bread to sizzle, drop heaping tablespoons of the onion mixture into the pan and cook for 1 to 2 minutes or until golden brown. Turn the fritters over and cook on the other side for about 1 to 2 minutes or until cooked through. Drain on paper towels and keep warm on a cookie sheet in the preheated onion. Repeat with remaining batter. Make a few fritters at a time; do not crowd the pan. Serve with the Sambal-Yogurt Dip.

Yield: Makes about 2 dozen fritters

STICKY WINGS

These wings are sweet, hot, and sticky! Watch people chomp on them, then lick off their fingers and the corners of their mouth to get every last drop of sauce. For football parties? Sure! But also any time you're entertaining casually. Be sure to offer plenty of napkins.

16 chicken wings
6 tablespoons (90 g) ketchup
3 tablespoons (45 g) sriracha
2 tablespoons (30 ml) apple cider vinegar
2 tablespoons (30 ml) soy sauce
3 tablespoons (60 g) honey
1 teaspoon chopped fresh ginger
1 large clove garlic, chopped
1/4 teaspoon ground cumin

Preheat the oven to 400°F (200°C, or gas mark 6). Wash the wings and separate the parts (discard the tips or use them for stock or bake them along with the other parts so you can nibble on them for extras). Line a baking sheet with aluminum foil and lightly oil the foil.

In a large bowl, combine the ketchup, sriracha, vinegar, soy sauce, honey, ginger, garlic, and cumin. Mix the ingredients to blend them thoroughly. Add the wings and coat them completely. Place the wings in a single layer on the baking sheet. Bake for 15 minutes.

Turn the wings over, brush with any remaining marinade and bake for another 15 minutes or until the wings are crispy.

Yield: Makes 32 pieces

WHITE BEAN, SUN-DRIED TOMATO, GOAT CHEESE, AND AVOCADO BRUSCHETTA

(D)

These are colorful, and you can make the toasts and topping several hours ahead of time (but keep the topping refrigerated) and put it all together at the last moment.

1 can (15 ounces, or 440 g) white beans, rinsed and drained

4 ounces (115 g) crumbled goat cheese or feta cheese

3 tablespoons (10.5 g) chopped sun-dried tomatoes

½ ripe avocado, cut into small dice

¼ cup (25 g) chopped kalamata olives

¼ cup (10 g) chopped fresh basil

1 large clove garlic, finely chopped

6 tablespoons (60 to 90 ml) olive oil, divided

French bread

Chop the beans coarsely and place them in a bowl. Add the cheese, tomatoes, avocado, olives, basil, garlic, and 4 tablespoons (60 ml) olive oil in a bowl. If the mixture seems dry, add a few drops more olive oil. Slice the bread into ¼- to ⅜-inch (6-mm to 1-cm)-thick slices. Brush lightly with the remaining 2 tablespoons (30 ml) olive oil. Toast the bread pieces lightly; they should be crispy but not browned. Spoon heaping tablespoons of the bean mixture on top of each toast.

Yield: Makes about 30 toasts

SERVING SUGGESTIONS AND VARIATIONS: This recipe is versatile. I've varied it from time to time, using kidney beans instead of white beans and blue cheese instead of goat or feta cheese. You can also include some capers.

SOUPS

There's a reason why the first known restau-
rants served only soup. It's because soup
soothes, satisfies, and comforts. Whether it is
a hot, thick chowder that warms you up (think
liquid electric blanket) or a cold potage that
offers relief from summer's heat, soup is a
restorative (the word at the foundation of
restaurant). This chapter has both hot and
cold soups, mild and spicy ones, some that
are first courses, and some that are satisfying
enough as full meals.

CARROT SOUP WITH HARISSA AND COCONUT

(P)

My husband Ed once declared this "the best dish I ever had."
The flavors are intriguing—there's heat from harissa, but coconut
milk to tame the spiciness and whole, fragrant cloves to give
it that mysterious "something."

2 tablespoons (30 ml) vegetable oil

1 medium onion, chopped

2 medium cloves garlic, chopped

1½ pounds (680 g) carrots, peeled and sliced

4 cups (950 ml) vegetable stock

6 whole cloves

1½ teaspoons (7.5 g) harissa

1 cup (235 ml) coconut milk

Salt, to taste

Shredded and toasted coconut, for garnish, optional

TIP

Canned coconut milk is thicker and more concentrated than refrigerator case coconut milk. You can use either here but I prefer the canned kind for this soup.

Heat the vegetable oil in a saucepan over medium heat. Add the onion and cook for 2 to 3 minutes. Add the garlic and carrots and cook briefly. Add the stock and cloves, bring to a boil, lower the heat, cover the pan partially, and cook for 25 minutes or until the carrots are soft. Remove the cloves. Purée the soup in a food processor or blender (or use a hand blender). Return the soup to the pan. Whisk in the harissa. Stir in the coconut milk. Bring the soup to a simmer. Cook for 10 minutes. Taste for seasoning and add salt to taste. Serve garnished with toasted coconut if desired.

Yield: Makes 6 servings

DID YOU KNOW? Hot and spicy ingredients such as harissa need some balance in a dish, otherwise you're just tasting pepper. Cool, rich, sweet ingredients such as coconut milk do the trick.

KALE AND WHITE BEAN SOUP WITH EGG AND CHEESE

(D)

This hearty soup is comfort food on a cold or snowy day. It's healthy, too, loaded with kale and beans. I've included eggs in this version to make it even more substantial, enough for a light supper.

1 pound (455 g) kale

2 tablespoons (30 g) olive oil

1 large onion, chopped

2 cans (15 ounces, or 425 g, each) cannellini beans

6 cups (1.4 L) vegetable stock

Salt and freshly ground black pepper, to taste

4 large eggs

4 slices Italian-style bread, cut 1 inch (2.5 cm) thick

1/2 cup (50 g) freshly grated Parmesan cheese

Wash the kale leaf by leaf to remove any dirt or sand. Remove and discard the thick stems. Cut the leaves and thin stems into shreds. Set aside. In a large saucepan, heat the olive oil over medium heat. Add the onion and cook for 3 to 4 minutes or until softened and beginning to brown. Mash half the beans and add them to the pan. Add the stock and bring to a boil. Add the kale, remaining beans, and salt and pepper to taste. Reduce the heat to a simmer, cover the pan partially, and cook for 20 minutes.

Beat the eggs. Gently pour small portions of the beaten egg into the soup in different places around the pan. Do not stir for 2 minutes. While the eggs are cooking, toast the bread. Stir the soup and ladle it into serving bowls. Top with the toast and sprinkle with cheese.

Yield: Makes 4 servings

DID YOU KNOW? Kale is a member of the cabbage family so it has a sharp, robust, almost bitter flavor. There are two basic varieties: flat leaf and curly leaf. Either is fine for this soup. Always remove the thick stems before using kale in recipes.

CHICKEN SOUP WITH CURRY AND APPLE

(M)

This is a dish that keeps people guessing because the flavors are so complex. I have several kinds of curry blends in my cabinet, but for this soup, I like one that isn't too hot and spicy.

2 tablespoons (30 ml) vegetable oil

1 medium onion, chopped

1 stalk celery, chopped

3 tablespoons (24 g) flour

2 teaspoons curry powder

1/8 teaspoon cayenne pepper

Salt and freshly ground black pepper, to taste

1 Golden Delicious apple, peeled and chopped

4 cups (950 ml) chicken stock

1 1/2 cups (337.5 g) finely shredded cooked chicken

1/2 cup (120 ml) coconut milk

Mango chutney and/or grated coconut, for garnish (optional)

Heat the vegetable oil in a saucepan over medium heat. Add the onion and celery and cook for 2 minutes, stirring occasionally. Stir in the flour, curry powder, cayenne, salt, and pepper. Add the apple and cook briefly. Gradually add the stock, stir, and bring to a simmer. Cook for 15 minutes.

Purée the soup in a food processor or blender (or use a hand blender). Return the soup to the pan. Add the chicken and coconut milk. Cook for 3 to 4 minutes or until heated through. Serve garnished with chutney and coconut, if desired.

Yield: Makes 4 to 6 servings

SERVING SUGGESTIONS AND VARIATIONS: You can serve this soup hot or cold. I prefer it without garnish, but serve the mango chutney and grated coconut for guests. Golden Delicious apples are widely available and gently sweet enough for this dish, but you can also use Honeycrisps.

DID YOU KNOW? Curry powder isn't a specific spice—it's a blend of spices typically used in East Indian cuisine. Most curry mixtures include chili powder, cumin, turmeric, cardamom, cinnamon, cloves, and coriander. Depending on the mix, the blend can be spicy-hot or on the warm/sweet side.

BLUEBERRY SOUP

(D)

When seasonal blueberries are in abundance I use them for pies and crisps, muffins and pancakes. But I also love their tart-sweet taste for soups such as this one, which I serve cold as a first course during the dog days of summer. The color, a rich, jewel-like magenta, is a wow. A good dish for company.

2 cups (290 g) blueberries

1/2 cups (355 ml) water

2 tablespoons (40 g) honey

1 cinnamon stick, 2 inches (5 cm) long

6 whole cloves

1 strip orange peel, 2 inches (5 cm) long

3/4 cup (115 g) plain yogurt, plus additional for topping, if desired

1/2 cup (120 ml) orange juice

2 tablespoons (30 ml) balsamic vinegar

Mint sprigs, optional

TIP

Use a muslin spice bag or a small piece of cheesecloth to wrap the cinnamon stick and cloves so you can remove them more easily.

Combine the blueberries, water, honey, cinnamon stick, cloves, and orange peel in a saucepan. Bring to a boil, lower the heat, and simmer for about 12 minutes. Remove and discard the cinnamon, cloves, and orange peel. Purée the soup in a food processor or blender (or use a hand blender). Return the soup to the pan. Refrigerate the soup until cold. Add the yogurt, orange juice, and balsamic vinegar and whisk the ingredients until thoroughly blended. Serve topped with mint sprigs and/or a blob of yogurt.

Yield: Makes 4 servings

SERVING SUGGESTIONS AND VARIATIONS: Serve these in small shot glasses as appetizers.

DID YOU KNOW? Some people believe that blueberries and huckleberries are the same. Although they look similar, they are different: Huckleberries have hard seeds, whereas blueberries have soft seeds, making them easier to use for recipes such as this one.

CREAM OF BEET SOUP WITH PUMPERNICKEL CRUMBLES

(D)

It takes an extra hour to roast the beets for this recipe, but it's absolutely worth the time because roasting them brings out the intense, concentrated, sweet flavor that stars in this dish. Pumpernickel crumbles are a terrific hearty and savory contrast. If you can't find pumpernickel, use rye bread instead.

3 large or 4 to 5 medium beets	1 teaspoon (2.7 g) grated fresh ginger
2 tablespoons (30 ml) olive oil	1/2 teaspoon ground cumin
1 tablespoon (14 g) butter	Salt and freshly ground black pepper, to taste
1 medium onion, chopped	5 cups (1.2 L) water
1 tart apple, peeled and chopped	1 cup (235 ml) whipping cream
2 cloves garlic, chopped	2 slices pumpernickel bread

Preheat the oven to 450°F (230°C, or gas mark 8). Scrub the beets and wrap them in a large piece of aluminum foil. Roast for about 1 hour or until tender. When the beets are cool enough to handle, remove the skins and cut them into small chunks.

Heat the olive oil and butter together in a large saucepan over medium heat. When the butter has melted and looks foamy, add the onion, apple, garlic, and ginger and cook for 5 to 6 minutes or until tender and beginning to brown. Add the cumin, salt, and pepper and stir. Add the beets to the pan. Add the water, bring to a simmer, and cook for about 20 minutes.

Purée the soup in a food processor or blender (or use a hand blender). Return the soup to the pan and stir in the cream. Heat through. Toast the pumpernickel and crumble the slices into small pieces. Serve the soup garnished with the pumpernickel crumbs.

Yield: Makes 4 to 6 servings

SERVING SUGGESTIONS AND VARIATIONS: This soup is gorgeous and makes a nice company dish whether you are serving a meat, dairy, or vegetarian meal. You can easily change it from dairy to parve by using Earth Balance Buttery Spread or margarine instead of butter, and coconut or soy milk instead of cream.

FISH SOUP WITH RICE NOODLES ⓟ

As of this writing, no kosher version exists for nam pla, the fish sauce usually made with fermented anchovies and used in Southeast Asian recipes. There is a hekhshered tuna-based fish sauce (available online, see page 15), but until an anchovy version becomes available, kosher cooks must adapt. Fish sauce basically consists of anchovies, salt, sugar, and water, which is what I used for this elegant Penang-style dish.

2 tablespoons (30 ml) vegetable oil

2 stalks lemongrass, chopped (about 2 tablespoons, or 12 g)

2 teaspoons finely chopped fresh ginger

1 or 2 small serrano or habanero chile peppers, deseeded and chopped

3 scallions, chopped

2 medium carrots, finely chopped

2 tablespoons (2 g) chopped fresh cilantro

3 cups (710 ml) fish or vegetable stock

3 cups (710 ml) coconut milk

3 anchovies, mashed

12 whole cloves

1/4 teaspoon ground turmeric

4 ounces (115 g) rice noodles, preferably spaghetti shape

1 pound (455 g) firm white fish (such as cod) cut into small chunks

1 cup (250 g) diced (3/4 inch, or 1.9 cm) firm tofu

2 to 3 tablespoons (30 to 45 ml) lime juice, to taste

Heat the vegetable oil in a large saucepan over medium heat. Add the lemongrass, ginger, chile pepper, scallions, carrots, and cilantro. Cook, stirring, for 2 to 3 minutes. Pour in the stock and coconut milk. Add the anchovies, cloves, and turmeric, stir and bring to a simmer. Cook for 15 minutes. Add the rice noodles and cook for 9 to 10 minutes. Add the fish and tofu and cook for 4 to 5 minutes or until the fish cooks through and the pasta is tender. Remove the pan from the heat, taste for seasoning, and stir in the lime juice to taste. Remove the cloves before serving.

Yield: Makes 4 servings

SUBSTITUTIONS AND VARIATIONS: Any firm white fish will do for this dish: scrod, tilapia, halibut, hake.

KIT CARSON SOUP

(D)

This hearty, nourishing soup has an interesting name. The original version was called Bowl of the Wife of Kit Carson, a specialty of The Fort restaurant in Denver. I suppose it got its name from some of the ingredients, which are indigenous to the Southwest. It was based on chicken stock, but I've made it vegetarian. And I've made so many other changes that I felt it could no longer be Kit Carson's wife's soup, so I renamed it and gave the old American frontiersman the credit.

2 tablespoons (30 ml) olive oil

1 medium onion, chopped

1 large clove garlic, chopped

1 chipotle pepper in adobo sauce, chopped

2 medium tomatoes, chopped (or 1 pint [473 ml] grape tomatoes, halved)

1 teaspoon (2.5 g) ground cumin

1 teaspoon (1 g) dried oregano

8 cups (2 L) vegetable stock

½ cup (97.5 g) white rice, uncooked

1 can (15 ounces, or 425 g) kidney beans, rinsed and drained

1 cup (165 g) corn kernels

Salt and freshly ground black pepper, to taste

1 ripe avocado, peeled and sliced

Taco chips

6 ounces (170 g) shredded Cheddar or Monterey Jack Cheese

Heat the olive oil in a soup pot over medium heat. Add the onion and cook for 2 to 3 minutes. Add the garlic, chipotle pepper, and tomatoes and cook for 1 to 2 minutes. Stir in the cumin and oregano. Pour in the stock. Bring the liquid to a boil, lower the heat, cover the pan, and simmer for 15 minutes. Add the rice, beans, and corn, cover and cook for 18 minutes. Taste for seasoning and add salt and pepper. Serve each bowl of soup with 2 to 3 taco chips on top, leaving room in the center. Scatter the cheese in the center, then add the avocado slices on top.

Yield: Makes 8 servings

SERVING SUGGESTIONS AND VARIATIONS: This soup is fine without the avocado and chips if you don't want to bother, and if you leave out the cheese the soup becomes parve. But do try it the authentic way first; it can be a full meal if you serve it with a crusty chunk of bread.

FRESH TOMATO VEGETABLE SOUP   Ⓓ

Like so many other kids, I grew up loving that staple of all lunch staples: grilled cheese with tomato soup. The sandwich was always fresh, the soup always canned. But canned soup changed over the years. Or maybe I did. So I always make my own now. Sometimes I make the creamy kind, but more often, I add extra vegetables and keep it chunky, like this one.

2 tablespoons (30 ml) vegetable oil

1 medium onion, chopped

2 stalks celery, sliced

2 carrots, sliced

1 small red bell pepper, deseeded and chopped

2 cloves garlic, chopped

3 pounds (1.4 kg) tomatoes, chopped

1 teaspoon (4.7 g) s'chug

3 tablespoons (12 g) chopped fresh parsley

2 teaspoons (2 g) fresh thyme leaves

4 cups (950 ml) vegetable stock

Salt and freshly ground black pepper, to taste

6 tablespoons (147 g) uncooked white rice

1 medium zucchini, cut into bite-size pieces

1 cup (230 g) plain yogurt or 1 cup (100 g) grated Parmesan cheese

Heat the vegetable oil in a soup pot over medium heat. Add the onion and cook for 2 to 3 minutes or until softened. Add the celery, carrots, bell pepper, and garlic and cook for 1 to 2 minutes. Add the tomatoes, s'chug, parsley, and thyme. Pour in the stock, season with salt and pepper, and bring the soup to a simmer. Cover the pan and cook for 10 minutes. Add the rice to the pan, cover and cook for another 10 minutes. Add the zucchini and cook for another 10 minutes or until the rice is tender. Serve hot with a dollop of yogurt or grated Parmesan cheese on top.

Yield: Makes 4 servings

SERVING SUGGESTIONS AND VARIATIONS: Yogurt is a pleasant contrast to the intense vegetable flavors of this dish, but it isn't essential. If you need a nondairy soup, skip the yogurt.

DID YOU KNOW? S'chug and harissa are just two of a multitude of spicy, chile pepper–based condiments that you can use to jazz up dishes like this soup. They are both more paste-like than sriracha or other hot sauces such as Tabasco. This soup is so versatile you can use any of these (or other similar condiments).

THANKSGIVING STUFFING SOUP (P)

I call this Thanksgiving Stuffing Soup because so many of the ingredients remind me of the ones I use for Thanksgiving turkey stuffing: chestnuts, onions, celery, herbs, and bread. But it contains no turkey or any other meat. It is a lush, thick, parve soup that's perfect as a first course for Thanksgiving dinner or any other time.

For the Soup:

2 tablespoons (30 ml) olive oil

1 medium onion, chopped

2 stalks celery, chopped

4 ripe pears, peeled and sliced

1 sprig of fresh thyme or 1 teaspoon fresh thyme leaves

Salt and freshly ground black pepper, to taste

3 cups (about 20 ounces, or 560 g) whole peeled roasted chestnuts

4 cups (950 ml) vegetable stock

1 cup (235 ml) water

1 cup (235 ml) almond milk

For the Herb Croutons:

3 tablespoons (45 ml) olive oil

3 cups (90 g) diced Italian bread, ciabatta, or home-style white bread

2 tablespoons (5 g) finely chopped fresh herbs

Salt, to taste

Make the Soup: Heat the olive oil in a large saucepan over medium heat. Add the onion and celery and cook, stirring occasionally, for 4 to 5 minutes or until softened. Add the pears and thyme, sprinkle with salt and pepper, and cook for about 2 minutes. Add the chestnuts, stock, and water. Raise the heat to high, and bring the liquid to a boil. Reduce the heat and simmer for 15 minutes or until vegetables and fruit are soft. Purée the soup in a food processor or blender (or use a hand blender). Return the soup to the pan. Stir in the almond milk and heat through. Taste for seasoning and add salt and pepper to taste. Serve with Herb Croutons.

Make the Herb Croutons: Heat the olive oil in a sauté pan over medium-low heat. Add the bread dice and herbs. Sprinkle with salt to taste and cook, turning frequently, for 4 to 5 minutes or until lightly browned.

Yield: Makes 6 servings

DID YOU KNOW? Freshly roasted chestnuts are an awesome-tasting snack, but packaged chestnuts are just fine for soup, and there are several kosher brands to choose from. Be sure to buy plain, roasted chestnuts for this recipe, not chestnuts in syrup.

ROASTED ASPARAGUS SOUP

(P)

Roasting the asparagus first makes them intensely flavorful.

1½ pounds (680 g) asparagus

½ cup (80 g) chopped shallots
or leeks (white part only)

2 tablespoons (30 ml) olive oil

Salt and freshly ground black
pepper, to taste

4 cups (950 ml) vegetable stock

1½ teaspoons chopped
fresh tarragon

½ cup (120 ml) coconut or soy milk

TIP

This recipe is easier if you use skinny or medium asparagus stalks; thick asparagus need peeling (the skins are too fibrous for puréeing).

Preheat the oven to 425°F (220°C, or gas mark 7). Line a large cookie sheet with parchment paper.

Trim the woody ends from the asparagus. Wash and dry the stalks and cut them into chunks. Place the asparagus pieces on the cookie sheet. Scatter the shallots onto the cookie sheet. Pour the olive oil over the vegetables and toss to coat them evenly. Sprinkle with salt and pepper to taste. Roast for 15 to 18 minutes or until the vegetables are tender and lightly browned.

Remove the vegetables from the oven and place in a saucepan. Add the stock and tarragon. Bring the soup to a boil, lower the heat, cover the pan partially, and cook for 10 to 12 minutes.

Purée the soup in a food processor or blender (or use a hand blender). Return the soup to the pan. Stir in the coconut milk and heat through. Serve hot, or refrigerate until thoroughly chilled and serve cold.

Yield: Makes 4 servings

SERVING SUGGESTIONS AND VARIATIONS: You can serve this soup hot or cold.

SALADS

A salad can be the most interesting part of a meal—or it can be the meal. Put together greens, fruits, vegetables, whole grains, meats, fish, tofu, dairy items, and dozens of other flavor-and-texture enhancing ingredients, toss with dressing, and you've got a salad that's also the meal. The recipes in this chapter include a light, refreshing pre-dinner salad (Baby Greens with Dried Figs, Pears, and Goat Cheese); a whole grain salad that's useful when you have leftovers (Freekeh Salad with Chicken, Mango, and Sugar Snaps); and a quick side dish that you can make in minutes when you're pressed for time (White Bean and Vegetable Hurry-Up Salad).

BABY GREENS WITH DRIED FIGS, PEARS, AND GOAT CHEESE

With its bright green spinach leaves, a blush of radicchio, and cool white goat cheese, this is a beautiful dish. It's a good, light first course, although I sometimes eat this as my lunch. The nuts aren't essential but add a nice crunch.

6 ounces (170 g) baby spinach

6 to 8 radicchio leaves, torn into bite-size pieces

1 large ripe pear

6 dried figs, chopped

1/2 cup (75 g) crumbled goat cheese

2 tablespoons (30 ml) olive oil

2 tablespoons (30 ml) balsamic vinegar

Salt and freshly ground black pepper, to taste

1/4 cup (35 g) chopped toasted almonds, optional

Wash and dry the spinach and place the leaves in a bowl. Add the radicchio leaves. Peel the pear, remove the seeds and core, chop into bite-size pieces, and add to the greens. Add the figs and cheese.

Pour the olive oil over the ingredients and toss to coat them evenly. Pour in the balsamic vinegar and add salt and pepper to taste. Toss the ingredients again.

Place the salad in a bowl or individual salad dishes and garnish with the almonds, if desired.

Yield: Makes 4 to 6 servings

SERVING SUGGESTIONS AND VARIATIONS: For a parve version, leave out the cheese.

FREEKEH SALAD WITH CHICKEN, MANGO, AND SUGAR SNAPS

Ⓜ

When it comes to salad, whole grains act like pasta and rice: They give bulk and substance. Add this or that—leftover chicken or crumbled cheese, some cooked or raw vegetables, dried fruit, nuts, and so on—and you've got a great side dish or main course. All that's needed is a good vinaigrette and you're done.

1 cup (228 g) whole-grain freekeh (or use farro, spelt, or oat groats)

1¾ cups (410 ml) water or chicken stock

1 cup (125 g) cut-up sugar snap peas

2 cups (280 g) cooked, diced chicken

1 ripe mango, peeled and diced

3 scallions, chopped

¼ cup (15 g) chopped fresh parsley

2 tablespoons (12 g) chopped fresh mint

1 teaspoon (2 g) grated fresh orange peel

Pinch ground cloves

¼ cup (60 ml) olive oil

2 tablespoons (30 ml) orange juice

2 tablespoons (30 ml) lemon juice or white wine vinegar

Salt and freshly ground black pepper, to taste

Place the freekeh and water or stock in a saucepan over high heat. Bring the liquid to a boil, stir, cover the pan, and lower the heat to a simmer. Cook for 35 to 40 minutes or until the grains are tender but still somewhat firm. Drain any liquid that has not been absorbed. Remove the pan from the heat, lift the cover, and place the sugar snap peas on top of the cooked grain. Cover the pan and set aside to cool. Place the cooked freekeh and sugar snaps in a bowl. Add the chicken, mango, scallions, parsley, mint, orange peel, and cloves. Toss to distribute the ingredients evenly. Combine the olive oil, orange and lemon juice and pour over the salad. Toss the ingredients again. Add salt and pepper to taste. Let rest for 15 minutes before serving.

Yield: Makes 4 to 6 servings

SERVING SUGGESTIONS AND VARIATIONS: This dish is incredibly flexible. For a dairy dish, substitute a firm cheese for the chicken. Add cooked vegetables instead of mango. Mix in crunchy water chestnuts or cashew nuts. If you don't have orange juice, use more white wine vinegar.

KALE, AVOCADO, AND FARRO SALAD WITH MARCONA ALMONDS ⓟ

Kale has become a big deal in the past couple of years, a favorite of people of all ages, including kids (kale chips anyone?), meat-eaters, and vegetarians alike. It's so good and useful I've wondered why it took so long to become popular. Although most recipes use cooked kale, we actually like it uncooked, in salad.

1 cup (190 g) farro

2 cups (475 ml) water

3 cups (210 g) chopped fresh kale

1 avocado

2 tablespoons (12 g) chopped fresh mint

2 tablespoons (30 ml) olive oil

Juice of one large lemon

1/3 cup (47 g) chopped marcona almonds

Place the farro and water in a saucepan and bring the liquid to a boil over high heat. Lower the heat, cover the pan and cook for about 25 to 30 minutes or until the farro is tender but still chewy. Drain any water that has not been absorbed. Place the cooked farro in a large bowl and let cool. Add the kale and toss the ingredients. Peel, pit, and cut the avocado into small chunks and add to the salad. Add the mint. Pour the olive oil over the ingredients and toss to distribute evenly. Pour in the lemon juice and toss. Add the almonds, toss once more, and serve.

Yield: Makes 6 servings

SERVING SUGGESTIONS AND VARIATIONS: You can make this dish with wheat berries, spelt, oat groats, freekeh, or kamut instead of farro.

DID YOU KNOW? All the positive press given to kale is certainly justified: It has plenty of nutritional benefits (it's loaded with antioxidant vitamins, calcium, and fiber), it's easy to prepare, and it has a compellingly tasty bitter edge.

OAT GROATS SALAD WITH ROASTED CAULIFLOWER, CARROTS, AND LIMA BEANS

(P)

Cooked oat groats make a terrific side dish in place of the more usual rice or potatoes. But more often than not I let the grains cool and use them for salad. They're so mild and versatile that I make a different version each time. This one includes carrots to highlight the grain's naturally sweet flavor, imported olives to add a tangy highlight, and lima beans to give it extra color.

1 cup (185 g) oat groats

2 cups (475 ml) water

1 cup sliced carrots (1/2 inch, or 1.3 cm, thick)

1 cup (100 g) cauliflower cut up
into bite-size pieces

4 tablespoons (30 ml) olive oil, divided

3/4 cup (124.5 g) frozen baby lima beans, thawed

1/3 cup (55 g) chopped red onion

1/2 cup (110 g) pitted black Niçoise olives, cut in half

3 tablespoons (45 ml) white wine vinegar

2 teaspoons fresh thyme leaves

Salt and freshly ground black pepper, to taste

Preheat the oven to 425°F (220°C, or gas mark 7). Place the oat groats in a saucepan, cover with the water, and bring to a boil over high heat. Turn the heat to low, cover the pan, and cook for about 25 minutes or until the groats are tender but still a bit chewy. Drain any water that has not been absorbed. Spoon the groats into a bowl. Place the carrots and cauliflower on a baking sheet. Pour about 1/2 tablespoon (7.5 ml) of the olive oil over the vegetables, toss to coat them, and roast for 15 minutes. Add the lima beans and red onion, toss with the carrots and cauliflower, and roast for another 5 minutes. Remove vegetables from the oven, let cool, and add to the cooked oat groats. Mix in the olives. Pour in the remaining olive oil and the white wine vinegar and toss to coat the ingredients. Sprinkle with thyme and season with salt and pepper. Toss the ingredients and let rest for at least 15 minutes before serving.

Yield: Makes 6 to 8 servings

SERVING SUGGESTIONS AND VARIATIONS: Use farro, spelt, or wheat berries instead of the oat groats; use peas or edamame in place of the lima beans.

QUINOA SALAD WITH FRESH FRUITS AND NUTS

(P)

Quinoa is an ancient grain-like crop that is relatively new to the kosher kitchen. And yet it has become a staple that I wonder what we ever did without it. When cooked, the grains make a light, but filling starch-like base for salads. But quinoa can be bitter, which means that sweet ingredients such as fruit are especially welcome mix-ins.

1 cup (173 g) quinoa
1½ cups (355 ml) water
1 large pear, peeled and diced
1 cup (150 g) quartered red seedless grapes
½ cup (70 g) chopped toasted almonds
3 tablespoons (18 g) chopped fresh mint
2 teaspoons chopped fresh ginger
1½ teaspoons chopped fresh rosemary
½ teaspoon ground cumin
2 tablespoons (30 ml) orange juice
1 tablespoon (15 ml) lime juice
3 tablespoons (45 ml) vegetable oil
Salt and freshly ground black pepper, to taste

TIP

Quinoa has a natural coating called saponin, which is what gives the grain its bitter taste. Many packages claim that the grains have been rinsed, but it's still a good idea to rinse quinoa for a minute or so under cold running water.

Place the quinoa in a strainer and rinse several times with cold water. Let drain. Bring the water to a boil in a saucepan, add the quinoa, bring to a boil, and stir. Lower the heat and simmer, covered, for about 15 minutes, or until all the liquid has been absorbed and the grains are tender. Remove the pan from the heat and spoon the quinoa into a bowl to cool. Add the pear, grapes, almonds, mint, ginger, rosemary, and cumin and toss to distribute the ingredients evenly. Mix the orange juice, lime juice, and vegetable oil together and pour over the salad. Toss the ingredients and let rest for 15 minutes before serving. Taste for seasoning and add salt and pepper.

Yield: Makes 4 to 6 servings

ROASTED BEET AND SQUASH SALAD WITH CITRUS AND HERBS

(P)

Beets and squash are both naturally sweet, and roasting them intensifies the sugary quality. Both are naturals for salad, too, because they go so well with so many different herbs, spices, seasonings, and salad dressings. Put them together to make a gorgeous garnet-red/autumn-orange presentation.

2 medium beets

1 small butternut squash

2 1/2 tablespoons (37.5 ml) olive oil, divided

Salt and freshly ground black pepper, to taste

1/4 cup (40 g) chopped red onion

2 tablespoons (8 g) chopped fresh dill

2 tablespoons (12 g) chopped fresh mint

1 tablespoon (6 g) grated fresh orange peel

2 tablespoons (15 g) lime juice

1 1/2 tablespoons (22.5 ml) white wine vinegar

TIP

If you buy beets with greens attached, remove the leaves, discard the thick stems, and cook the greens as you would spinach, kale, or chard. Always wear disposable gloves when working with beets to keep your hands from becoming stained from the natural red beet juices.

Preheat the oven to 425°F (220°C, or gas mark 7). Line a baking sheet with parchment paper. Trim the beets, cutting away the greens, if any, and discarding any hard, fibrous parts of the stem. Scrub the beets, wrap them in aluminum foil, and roast for 50 to 60 minutes or until they are tender. When the beets are cool enough to handle, peel them, cut them into bite-size pieces, and place in a bowl. About halfway through the beet roasting, cut the squash in half, scoop out the seeds and peel the halves. Cut the halves into chunks and place them on the baking sheet. Pour 1/2 tablespoon (7.5 ml) of the olive oil over the chunks, toss to coat them evenly, and sprinkle with salt and pepper. Roast for 25 to 30 minutes or until tender and lightly crispy. Remove the squash chunks and let cool. Combine the cooled squash with the beets. Add the onion, dill, mint, and orange peel. Pour in the remaining olive oil, lime juice, and vinegar. Toss the ingredients and let rest for about 15 minutes before serving.

Yield: Makes 6 servings

GRILLED MARINATED SALMON AND COUSCOUS SALAD

(P)

I use fresh salmon for this dish, but in a pinch you can make it with canned salmon. It's a good choice for brunch as well as lunch or even a light dinner.

1/2 cup (120 ml) olive oil, divided

3 tablespoons (45 ml) white wine vinegar

11/2 teaspoons Dijon mustard

11/2 tablespoons (22.5 ml) soy sauce

1 medium clove garlic, finely chopped

1/2 teaspoon crushed red pepper

1 pound (115 g) boneless salmon, about 11/4 inches (3 cm) thick

2 cups (350 g) Israeli couscous

1 cup (165 g) frozen peas, thawed

3 scallions, chopped

2 tablespoons (30 ml) orange juice

2 tablespoons (30 ml) lemon juice

Salt and freshly ground black pepper, to taste

Combine 1/4 cup (60 ml) olive oil, the vinegar, mustard, soy sauce, garlic, and red pepper in a non-reactive dish large enough to hold the salmon. Add the salmon, turning the fish to coat all sides with the marinade. Let marinate in the refrigerator for at least 1 hour. Grill or broil the fish for about 10 minutes or until cooked through. Let cool. Crumble the salmon into a bowl.

Cook the couscous according to the package directions. Add the cooked couscous to the bowl with the salmon. Add the peas and scallions and toss to distribute the ingredients evenly.

Mix the remaining 1/4 cup (60 ml) olive oil, orange juice, and lemon juice and pour over the salad. Season to taste with salt and pepper, toss the ingredients, and let rest for at least 15 minutes before serving.

Yield: Makes 4 servings

ROASTED LEMON-ROSEMARY POTATO SALAD

(P)

Almost everything my mom cooked tasted delicious, but I didn't love the way she made potato salad, so I've spent a lot of time trying to personalize my own. Over the years, I made more versions than I can count—in fact, I think I have a book's worth. Most of them begin with the usual steamed or poached potatoes. But this one, with crispy cubes of golden brown roasted potatoes, opened up an entire new vision of what potato salad could be.

3 pounds (1.4 kg) Yukon gold or California white potatoes

6 tablespoons (90 ml) olive oil, divided

Salt, to taste

4 scallions, chopped

1/4 cup (15 g) chopped fresh parsley

2 teaspoons chopped fresh rosemary

1 teaspoon grated lemon peel

2 tablespoons (30 ml) lemon juice

2 teaspoons Dijon mustard

Freshly ground black pepper, to taste

Preheat the oven to 425°F (220°C, or gas mark 7). Peel the potatoes and cut them into 1/2-inch (1.3 cm) dice. Line a baking sheet with parchment paper and place the potatoes on the paper. Pour 3 tablespoons (45 ml) of the olive oil over the potatoes, toss them to coat all sides, and sprinkle with salt. Roast the potatoes for about 30 minutes, turning them 2 to 3 times, until they are tender and crispy. Place the potatoes in a bowl. While the potatoes are still warm, add the scallions, parsley, rosemary, and lemon peel and toss the ingredients. Mix the remaining 3 tablespoons (45 ml) olive oil, lemon juice, and Dijon mustard. Pour over the potatoes. Toss the ingredients. Season to taste with salt and pepper. Let rest for at least 15 minutes before serving.

Yield: Makes 8 servings

SERVING SUGGESTIONS AND VARIATIONS: This dish is best when served warm or at room temperature, not cold. It's a good choice for buffet serving. You can halve the recipe easily for fewer servings.

KAMUT, CORN, AND TOMATO SALAD (P)

Kamut looks like fat brown rice but is actually related to wheat. It has a nutty flavor and pleasantly sturdy texture. I use it interchangeably with other whole grains (such as spelt, farro, and freekeh) for recipes such as this one.

1 cup (185 g) kamut

2 cups (475 ml) water

2 ears corn, cooked (about 1½ cups, or 245 g, kernels)

1 cup (180 g) cut-up grape tomatoes

1 cup (124 g) diced zucchini

3 to 4 scallions, chopped

1 tablespoon (4 g) chopped fresh oregano

2 tablespoons (30 ml) olive oil

1 tablespoon (15 ml) white wine vinegar

1 tablespoon (15 ml) lime juice

1 teaspoon Dijon mustard

Salt and freshly ground black pepper, to taste

Place the kamut in a bowl, cover with water, and soak for 1 hour.

Drain and place the kamut in a saucepan. Add the 2 cups (475 ml) water. Bring to a boil over high heat. Lower the heat, cover the pan, and cook for about 45 minutes or until the grains are tender but still slightly chewy. Drain any water that has not been absorbed. Place the kamut in a bowl. Add the corn, tomatoes, zucchini, scallions, and oregano and toss to distribute the ingredients evenly.

In a small bowl, combine the olive oil, white wine vinegar, lime juice, and mustard and whisk the ingredients to blend them thoroughly. Pour over the salad and toss. Let rest for at least 15 minutes before serving. Taste for seasoning and add salt and pepper.

Yield: Makes 6 servings

SERVING SUGGESTIONS AND VARIATIONS: You can change this recipe in so many ways. Add chopped cooked vegetables such as carrots, roasted asparagus, or thawed frozen peas; add other flavor ingredients such as kalamata olives; and add cheese (feta and goat are particularly delicious with this dish) for a dairy meal.

WHITE BEAN AND VEGETABLE HURRY-UP SALAD

I call this a "hurry-up" salad because I can make it quickly using staple items I always have in the house: cans of white beans in the cabinet; peas in the freezer; cumin on the spice shelf; avocados and carrots in the bin; and fresh parsley, mint, and lemon in the crisper drawer. It's a colorful dish that I have used both for family dinner and buffets when I have casual company meals.

1 can (15 ounces, or 425 g) white beans	1/4 cup (24 g) chopped fresh mint
3 medium carrots, sliced thin	1 teaspoon ground cumin
1 ripe avocado, peeled and chopped	1/8 teaspoon cayenne pepper
1 cup (130 g) frozen peas, thawed	1/4 cup (60 ml) olive oil
1/2 cup (80 g) chopped red onion	3 tablespoons (45 ml) lemon juice
1/4 cup (15 g) chopped fresh parsley	Salt, to taste

Rinse the white beans under cold running water; let drain and place them in a bowl. Add the carrots, avocado, peas, onion, parsley, mint, cumin, and cayenne pepper and toss to distribute the ingredients evenly.

Pour in the olive oil and lemon juice. Toss again to coat the ingredients. Taste for seasoning and add salt to taste. Let rest for about 15 minutes before serving.

Yield: Makes 6 servings

SERVING SUGGESTIONS AND VARIATIONS: Use chickpeas or black beans instead of white beans; use any cooked chopped green vegetable (such as broccoli, green string beans, thawed frozen lima beans, or edamame) instead of peas.

LENTIL AND SEARED TOMATO AND ARUGULA SALAD

French green lentils are the upscale, high-class kind; in fact, they have been called "poor man's caviar." They have a rich, mineral-y flavor and, unlike most other lentil varieties, stay firm after cooking, making them ideal for salad.

1 cup (192 g) French green lentils
3 tablespoons (45 ml) olive oil, divided
2 cups (360 g) halved grape tomatoes
3 to 4 scallions, chopped
2 cups (40 g) chopped fresh arugula
2 tablespoons (30 ml) white wine vinegar
1/2 teaspoon Dijon mustard
Salt and freshly ground black pepper, to taste

Place the lentils in a saucepan, cover with water by at least 2 inches (5 cm), and bring to a boil over high heat. Reduce the heat to a simmer, cover the pan, and cook the lentils until they are tender, about 20 minutes. Drain the lentils and place them in a bowl.

Heat 1 tablespoon (15 ml) of the olive oil in a sauté pan over medium heat. Add the tomatoes and scallions and cook for about 2 minutes or until softened. Add the arugula, cook briefly just until wilted. Spoon the contents of the pan into the bowl with the lentils.

Mix the remaining 2 tablespoons (30 ml) olive oil, white wine vinegar, and mustard and pour over the salad ingredients. Season to taste with salt and pepper and toss the ingredients. Let rest for at least 15 minutes before serving.

Yield: Makes 4 servings

4

GRAINS, BEANS, PASTA, AND VEGETARIAN DISHES

Years ago the prospect of making a vegetarian meal seemed odd, but no longer. More and more of us are going meatless—at least occasionally. And it seems at least one person in our family or among our friends is a vegetarian. The amazingly wide assortment of whole grains, beans, pasta, and produce now available makes cooking wholesome, interesting vegetarian dishes a lot easier for the kosher home cook than it used to be. This chapter includes recipes that can be used as side dishes (Quinoa-Stuffed Portobello Mushroom Caps with Raisins and Pine Nuts) or main courses (Roasted Vegetable Hash with Egg and Horseradish Crème Fraîche).

KALE AND POTATO GRATIN

(D)

Parents in America pack kale chips in their children's lunch boxes. Grownups are eating more of this dark, green-leaved vegetable, too. Who could have predicted that this cabbage cousin, once a relatively unknown and underused vegetable, would become so popular?

4 medium Yukon gold potatoes

1 large bunch kale (12 to 16 ounces, or 340 to 455 g)

4 tablespoons (56 g) butter, divided

2 tablespoons (16 g) all-purpose flour

1 3/4 cups (410 ml) whole milk

Salt and freshly ground black pepper, to taste

1/8 teaspoon freshly grated nutmeg, or to taste

1 cup (150 g) finely grated Swiss cheese

1/2 cup (30 g) packed fresh bread crumbs

2 to 3 tablespoons (10 to 15 g) grated Parmesan cheese

Preheat the oven to 400°F (200°C, or gas mark 6). Butter a baking dish. Peel the potatoes and boil them in lightly salted water for about 15 minutes or until tender. Let cool and slice. Place half the slices on the bottom of the baking dish. While the potatoes are cooking, wash the kale and remove the thick stems from the bottom. Chop the leaves and thin stems coarsely. Bring a large saucepan of water to a boil. Immerse the kale and cook for 7 to 8 minutes or until soft. Drain and squeeze out as much water as possible. Set the kale aside. Melt 2 tablespoons (28 g) butter in a saucepan over medium heat. When the butter has melted and looks foamy, add the flour and cook for about 1 minute, stirring constantly. Gradually add the milk and stir until the sauce is smooth and thick, about 2 minutes. Season to taste with salt, pepper, and nutmeg and stir to blend the ingredients. Add the Swiss cheese and mix it in. Stir in the kale. Spoon half the mixture into the prepared baking dish and spread to cover the potatoes. Repeat with remaining potatoes and kale mixture. Melt the remaining 2 tablespoons (28 g) butter, mix with the bread crumbs, and sprinkle over the kale. Top with the Parmesan cheese. Bake for 22 to 25 minutes or until hot and bubbly. Broil for a minute or so, if desired, for a brown crust.

Yield: Makes 6 servings

SERVING SUGGESTIONS AND VARIATIONS: You can make this using chard or spinach.

DID YOU KNOW? There are several types of kale, but we usually see two main kinds in the stores: curly kale and Lacinato (Dino, Tuscan). Curly kale is lively and peppery. Lacinato kale (best for chips) is somewhat sweeter and milder. You might also find Red Russian or other red kale varieties.

CHICKEN FRIED PORTOBELLO STEAK AND CHIVE EGGS

Chicken fried steak, which is a popular dish in the South, is a riff on southern fried chicken, only it's made with beef. This is my vegetarian version. It's made with seasoned and floured "meaty" portobello mushrooms cooked to golden brown, crunchy-crusted goodness.

4 large portobello mushrooms

1/2 cup (64 g) all-purpose flour, divided

10 large eggs, divided

1 tablespoon (15 ml) water

6 tablespoons (54 g) cornmeal

2 tablespoons (8 g) chopped fresh parsley

1/2 teaspoon dried sage

1/2 teaspoon garlic powder

1/4 teaspoon paprika

1/8 teaspoon cayenne pepper

Salt, to taste

Vegetable oil, for frying

3 tablespoons (9 g) chopped chives

1 tablespoon (15 ml) olive oil or (14 g) margarine

Rinse, trim, and dry the mushrooms. Place 1/4 cup (32 g) flour in a dish. Beat 2 eggs and water in a second dish. Mix the remaining 1/4 cup (32 g) flour, cornmeal, parsley, sage, garlic powder, paprika, cayenne, and salt in a third dish. Coat the portobellos with the flour. Dip each mushroom into the egg mixture, making sure to coat the entire surface. Then dip into the flour-cornmeal mixture, making sure to coat the entire surface. Place the mushrooms on a cake rack and let them air-dry for at least 15 minutes. Heat about 1/2 inch (1.3 cm) vegetable oil (enough to come halfway up the sides of the mushrooms) in a large sauté pan over medium-high heat. When the oil is hot enough to make a bread crumb sizzle, fry the mushrooms for about 3 minutes per side or until crispy and golden brown. Beat the remaining 8 eggs and the chives in a bowl. Heat the olive oil in a large sauté pan over medium heat. Add the eggs and cook them, stirring occasionally, until they are almost set but still glossy. Transfer the eggs to serving plates accompanied by a fried mushroom.

Yield: Makes 4 servings

SERVING SUGGESTIONS AND VARIATIONS: If the mushrooms are large enough, you can serve the eggs inside of them. If you prefer, fry the eggs in butter for a dairy meal.

EGGPLANT, TOMATO, AND MASHED POTATO GRATIN

(D)

This recipe began as Eggplant Parmesan and I gradually changed it—first by grilling the eggplant instead of breading and frying it, then by using fresh tomatoes instead of sauce, and then by adding layers—until it became something entirely different. I usually make this version because it is one of my daughter Meredith's favorites. Sometimes I substitute zucchini for the eggplant and chard for the spinach. This dish is very filling, so it works as a main course as well as a side dish.

2 large Yukon gold potatoes

1 tablespoon (14 g) butter

1 cup grated (150 g) Swiss cheese, divided

1/2 cup (50 g) grated Parmesan cheese, divided

3 large eggs

Salt and freshly ground black pepper, to taste

1 medium eggplant (or 2 medium zucchini)

6 tablespoons (90 ml) olive oil, divided

1 bunch spinach, washed and dried

2 large portobello mushroom caps

2 medium tomatoes

3 tablespoons (7.5 g) chopped fresh basil

2 tablespoons (7.5 g) chopped fresh parsley

TIP

You can make this dish a day or two ahead of serving time. Store, covered, in the refrigerator.

Peel the potatoes, cut them into chunks, and cook them in simmering water until tender, about 15 minutes. Drain the potatoes and mash them in the pot. Stir in the butter, 1/2 cup (75 g) Swiss cheese, 1/4 cup (25 g) Parmesan cheese, and the eggs. Mash the ingredients until the mixture is smooth. Season to taste with salt and pepper.

While the potatoes are cooking, preheat the oven broiler or outdoor grill. Trim the ends from the eggplant. Slice the eggplant (or zucchini) lengthwise into 1/4-inch (6-mm) slices. Sprinkle with salt and let rest for about 15 minutes. Wipe the surfaces dry with paper towels. Brush both sides of the eggplant slices using about 5 tablespoons (75 ml) of the olive oil. Broil or grill the eggplant for 2 to 3 minutes per side or until softened and lightly browned. Remove the eggplant from the broiler or grill and set aside.

Heat the remaining tablespoon (15 ml) of olive oil in a sauté pan over medium heat and cook the spinach for 3 to 4 minutes, or until wilted. Press out any liquid left in the spinach and set it aside.

Place half the eggplant slices in a rectangular baking dish. Cover with the mashed potato mixture. Place the spinach on top of the potatoes. Layer the remaining eggplant on top. Slice the mushroom caps about 1/4-inch (6-mm) thick and place them on top of the eggplant. Chop the tomatoes and mix them with the basil and parsley. Place them over the mushrooms. Sprinkle the remaining Swiss cheese and Parmesan cheese on top. Preheat the oven to 350°F (180°C, or gas mark 4). Cook for 45 minutes or until crispy and lightly browned on top.

Yield: Makes 8 servings

DID YOU KNOW? This is a useful family dairy main course during Passover.

FARFALLE NIÇOISE WITH ROASTED TOMATOES

(D)

This recipe first came about during the winter, when I was daydreaming about warmer weather. I thought a summery dish such as Salade Niçoise would be a mood lifter, but instead of making the salad, I used the ingredients in a heartier pasta dish. You don't have to save this for winter dining though.

3 cups (450 g) grape tomatoes

2 large cloves garlic, chopped

1 large onion, chopped

5 tablespoons (75 ml) olive oil, divided

Salt and freshly ground black pepper, to taste

1½ cups chopped green beans (about 1 inch, or 2.5 cm, pieces)

1 pound (455 g) farfalle pasta

3/4 cup (660 g) halved Niçoise or other olives

2 tablespoons (17 g) capers, rinsed

1/4 cup (10 g) chopped fresh basil

1 cup (100 g) grated fresh Parmesan cheese

Preheat the oven to 425°F (220°C, or gas mark 7). Line a baking sheet with foil or parchment paper. Wash and dry the tomatoes; cut them in half. Place the tomatoes on the baking sheet. Add the garlic and onion. Pour 3 tablespoons (45 ml) olive oil over the vegetables and toss to coat them. Sprinkle with salt and pepper. Roast for 15 minutes. Add the green beans, pour in 1 more tablespoon (15 ml) olive oil, mix the vegetables, and roast for another 10 to 12 minutes or until the green beans are crispy but tender. Remove the vegetables from the oven and set them aside.

Cook the pasta al dente. Reserve 1/4 cup (60 ml) pasta water. Drain the pasta, and add the roasted vegetables and their juices. Add the olives, capers, basil, and remaining tablespoon (15 ml) olive oil. Toss to distribute the ingredients evenly. Sprinkle with salt to taste. Add the pasta water if necessary for moister texture. Sprinkle with the cheese and serve.

Yield: Makes 4 servings

SERVING SUGGESTIONS AND VARIATIONS: This is a vegetarian main course, but you can make it into a fish dish by adding cut-up pieces of fresh grilled tuna or canned, drained tuna.

ROASTED VEGETABLE HASH WITH EGG AND HORSERADISH CRÈME FRAÎCHE

(D)

With its sunny-side egg yolk seeping into bits of golden brown crispy pieces, hash is the comfort food of comfort foods. Add toasted English muffins, warm pitas, or crusty focaccia and you can't ask for a more satisfying dinner or brunch dish. A jazzed-up, mildly spicy crème fraîche accompaniment makes this dish a good choice for company.

For the Roasted Vegetable Hash:

1 stalk broccoli

4 medium carrots, peeled and cut into 1/2-inch (1.3-cm) dice

4 medium Yukon gold potatoes, peeled and cut into 1/2-inch (1.3-cm) dice

2 medium parsnips, peeled and cut into 1/2-inch (1.3-cm) dice

1 large leek

4 tablespoons (60 ml) olive oil, divided

Salt and freshly ground black pepper, to taste

2 tablespoons (28 g) butter or margarine

1 cup (70 g) chopped mushrooms

1/2 cup (120 ml) vegetable stock (or cream)

3 tablespoons (9 g) chopped chives

8 to 12 eggs, sunny-side up

For the Horseradish Crème Fraîche:

1 cup (56 g) crème fraîche

3 tablespoons (45 g) prepared white horseradish

2 tablespoons (6 g) chopped chives or scallion tops

2 to 3 tablespoons (30 to 45 ml) cream or milk, optional

Make the Vegetable Hash: Preheat the oven to 400°F (200°C, or gas mark 6). Line a baking sheet with parchment paper. Rinse the broccoli and cut the top into small, bite-size pieces. Peel the stalk and cut it into bite-size pieces. Place the broccoli on the baking sheet. Add the carrots, potatoes, and parsnips.

Remove and discard the root and the green part of the leek. Slice the white part in half lengthwise, then rinse under cold running water to clean the leek thoroughly. Drain and chop the leek. Place the leek with the other vegetables on the baking sheet. Pour 3 tablespoons (45 ml) olive oil over the vegetables, toss to coat them completely. Sprinkle to taste with salt and pepper. Roast for about 25 minutes, stirring the vegetables occasionally, or until they are tender. Set aside.

Heat the butter and remaining tablespoon (15 ml) olive oil in a sauté pan over medium heat. When the butter has melted and looks foamy, add the mushrooms and cook for 1 minute. Add the roasted vegetables and cook, stirring and mashing them slightly, for another minute. Pour in the stock and add the chives. Stir to incorporate them into the vegetables. Cook, flipping the vegetables occasionally, for about 15 to 20 minutes or until browned and crispy.

Serve the hash topped with sunny-side up eggs and Horseradish Crème Fraîche.

Make the Horseradish Crème Fraîche: You can buy packaged crème fraîche in the dairy case of many supermarkets. This mixture takes just a few minutes. Serve it with this hash or with eggs; with smoked salmon frittata; with roasted beets; instead of cream cheese with bagels and smoked salmon; in potato salad; and with dozens of other dishes.

Combine the crème fraîche, horseradish, and chives in a bowl and whisk to a smooth consistency. Stir in the cream if you prefer a thinner sauce. Makes slightly more than 1 cup (285 g).

Yield: Makes 4 to 6 servings

SERVING SUGGESTIONS AND VARIATIONS: You can add additional soft vegetables (such as thawed frozen peas or diced zucchini) to the hash. Fry them for 1 to 2 minutes just before you place the roasted vegetables in the sauté pan. For a parve dish, serve the hash without the crème fraîche.

QUINOA-STUFFED PORTOBELLO MUSHROOM CAPS WITH RAISINS AND PINE NUTS

(P)

This makes such a gorgeous presentation that I save it for special occasions. It has lots of interesting texture elements and makes a good side dish or lunch dish. You can also use it as a first course at a Seder meal if you eat quinoa during Passover.

6 large portobello mushroom caps

3 tablespoons (45 ml) olive oil, divided

Salt and freshly ground black pepper, to taste

4 thick scallions, chopped

¼ cup (35 g) pine nuts

1 large clove garlic, chopped

¼ cup (35 g) golden raisins

2 cups (370 g) cooked quinoa

2 tablespoons (12 g) chopped fresh mint

Preheat the oven to 350°F (180°C, or gas mark 4). Wipe the mushroom caps clean, remove the inedible stems and place the caps outside up on a baking sheet. Brush the outsides with 1 tablespoon (15 ml) olive oil. Sprinkle with salt and pepper. Turn the caps over (the gills side up). Bake for 10 minutes or until softened.

While the caps are baking, heat the remaining 2 tablespoons (30 ml) olive oil in a sauté pan over medium heat. Add the scallions and pine nuts and cook for 1 to 2 minutes. Add the garlic and raisins and cook for another minute. Add the quinoa and mint; cook briefly and stir to distribute the ingredients evenly. Taste for seasoning and add salt and pepper.

Spoon equal amounts of the quinoa mixture into each mushroom cap. Just before serving, bake the caps for 10 to 12 minutes or until the mushrooms are tender.

Yield: Makes 6 servings

FARRO RISOTTO WITH WILD MUSHROOMS AND ASPARAGUS

(P)

If you're bored with rice and potatoes, try farro or some other whole grain instead. They open up a world of new side dishes. This dish is filling enough as a vegetarian main course.

1 cup (190 g) farro

2 cups (475 ml) water

4 tablespoons (60 ml) olive oil, divided

2 cups (140 g) chopped wild mushrooms

2 cups (270 g) chopped asparagus

1 medium onion, chopped

1/2 cup (120 ml) white wine

2 cups (475 ml) vegetable stock, heated

1/4 cup (15 g) chopped parsley

2 tablespoons (8 g) chopped fresh dill

Salt and freshly ground black pepper, to taste

Place the farro and water in a saucepan and bring to a boil over high heat. Lower the heat, cover the pan, and cook for 15 minutes. Drain the farro and set it aside.

Heat 2 tablespoons (30 ml) olive oil in a sauté pan over medium heat. Add the mushrooms and asparagus and cook, stirring, for 1 minute. Cover the pan and cook for another 2 to 3 minutes. Dish out the vegetables and set them aside.

Heat the remaining 2 tablespoons (30 ml) olive oil in the pan. Add the onion and cook, stirring, occasionally, for 2 to 3 minutes or until softened.

Add the farro and stir to mix the ingredients. Pour in the white wine and cook, stirring, for 3 to 4 minutes or until it has been absorbed. Gradually add the stock, continue to stir, and cook for about 10 minutes or until all the liquid has been absorbed. Add the vegetable mixture and stir to distribute the ingredients evenly. Mix in the parsley and dill and sprinkle with salt and pepper.

Yield: Makes 4 servings

SERVING SUGGESTIONS AND VARIATIONS: Make this into a dairy dish by sprinkling the top with 1/2 cup (75 g) grated Fontina, Parmesan, or Swiss cheese.

FARRO PILAF WITH SQUASH, EDAMAME, AND PUMPKIN SEEDS

(P)

This is a beautiful, colorful, and healthy side dish. Or main course. You choose! Although it's certainly filling enough for dinner (add a soup or salad), it is also ideal for those occasions, maybe a holiday dinner, when you're going to serve a roast but need a vegetarian dish or two.

2 cups (280 g) diced butternut squash
(about 1/2-inch, or 1.3-cm, cubes)

3 tablespoons (45 ml) vegetable oil, divided

Salt and freshly ground black pepper, to taste

1 cup (190 g) farro

13/4 cups (410 ml) vegetable stock

1 medium onion, chopped

1 cup (118 g) frozen edamame, thawed

2 tablespoons (7.5 g) chopped fresh parsley

6 tablespoons (60 g) toasted pumpkin seeds

> **TIP**
> Farro, which is a form of wheat, is best when tender but still chewy.

Preheat the oven to 400°F (200°C, or gas mark 6). Line a baking sheet with parchment paper. Place the squash on the paper, pour 1 tablespoon (15 ml) vegetable oil on top, and toss to coat all the pieces. Sprinkle with salt and pepper and bake for about 20 minutes, turning the pieces occasionally, or until they are tender and crispy. Remove from the oven and set aside. While the squash is roasting, place the farro and stock in a saucepan, bring to a boil over high heat, stir, lower the heat, cover the pan, and cook for 20 to 25 minutes or until tender but still chewy. Discard any remaining liquid. Remove the pan from the heat. Heat the remaining vegetable oil in a sauté pan over medium heat. Add the onion and cook for about 3 minutes, or until softened. Add the farro, squash, edamame, and parsley to the sauté pan with the onion; add salt and pepper to taste. Cook, tossing to distribute the ingredients evenly, for 2 to 3 minutes or until hot. Place in a serving dish, sprinkle with the pumpkin seeds, and serve.

Yield: Makes 4 to 6 servings

SERVING SUGGESTIONS AND VARIATIONS: Use any whole grain (such as spelt, wheat berries, oat groats, kamut, or freekeh). Peas can fill in for edamame.

FREEKEH AND VEGETABLE "MUJADARAH"

(P)

I once read that Mujadarah is the dish the biblical Esau thought so tempting and delicious that he sold his birthright for a bowlful. Well, maybe yes, maybe no, but it is so good that it has become one of our family favorites. And it is my go-to whenever I need an easy vegetarian dish (such as at our annual Yom Kippur break-the-fast). In the Middle East, Mujadarah is usually made with rice or bulgur wheat and lentils, but I like to mix the recipe up and use other grains and sometimes add vegetables.

1 cup (230 g) whole-grain freekeh

1 3/4 cups (410 ml) water or vegetable stock

6 tablespoons (90 ml) olive oil, divided

6 to 8 large yellow onions, peeled and sliced

1 cup (192 g) French green lentils

2 1/2 cups (570 ml) water

3 carrots, chopped into small pieces
(about 1/2 inch, or 1.3 cm)

4 cups (4 to 5 ounces, or 115 to 140 g) fresh spinach

1/2 cup (30 g) chopped fresh parsley

1 teaspoon ground cumin

Salt, to taste

TIP

Freekeh has a more satisfying texture when it's cooked al dente: about 35 minutes for the whole grain, about 20 minutes for the cracked grain.

Place the freekeh and water or stock in a saucepan over high heat. Bring the liquid to a boil, stir, cover the pan, and lower the heat to a simmer. Cook for about 30 to 35 minutes, or until the grains are tender but still somewhat firm and all the liquid has been absorbed. Remove from the heat and set aside to cool. Place the cooked freekeh in a bowl.

While the freekeh is cooking, heat 4 tablespoons (60 ml) olive oil in a large sauté pan over low-medium heat. Add the onions and cover the pan; cook, stirring occasionally, for 15 to 20 minutes or until the onions are soft and brown. Spoon the onions into a container and cover the container. Refrigerate when cool if not serving the dish immediately.

Place the lentils in a saucepan and cover with the 2 1/2 cups (570 ml) water. Bring to a boil over high heat. Lower the heat, cover the pan, and cook for 15 minutes. Add the carrots, cover the pan, and cook for another 10 minutes or until the carrots and lentils are tender. Remove the pan from the heat. Add the spinach, cover the pan, and let rest for a few minutes to wilt the greens.

Drain and place the lentils, carrots, and spinach in the bowl with the freekeh. Stir in the remaining 2 tablespoons (30 ml) olive oil. Add the parsley and toss the ingredients. Add the cumin and salt.

Stir in the onions with any accumulated juices and serve. If serving at a later time, stir in the onions and juices, place in a baking dish, cover, and refrigerate. When ready to serve, reheat in a preheated 350°F (180°C, or gas mark 4) oven.

Yield: Makes 4 servings

....

DID YOU KNOW? Freekeh is immature wheat harvested while still green. After harvest, the grain is roasted to bring out a nutty, smoky flavor. It may be a hot new item at the market, but freekeh was known in ancient times; in fact, it is mentioned in Leviticus 2:14. This grain is a nutritional power-house—high protein, high fiber, low on the glycemic index, and a good source of calcium and iron.

VEGETABLE POT PIE

(P)

Although we're a family of meat eaters, we've eaten more vegetarian meals in the past few years. Chalk it up to changing styles and tastes. This dish began as chicken pot pie. Now, minus the poultry and plus broccoli and winter squash, it's still somewhat familiar and just as filling as the original.

2 medium all-purpose potatoes, peeled and cut into bite-size pieces

2 carrots, sliced 1/2-inch (1.3-cm) thick

1 cup (140 g) chopped butternut squash (bite-size pieces)

1 cup (71 g) chopped broccoli (bite-size pieces)

2 tablespoons (30 ml) olive oil

1 medium onion, chopped

1 clove garlic, chopped

1 cup (164 g) frozen corn kernels

2 tablespoons (7.5 g) chopped fresh parsley

2 teaspoons (2 g) fresh thyme leaves

Salt and freshly ground black pepper, to taste

2 1/2 tablespoons (20 g) all-purpose flour

1 1/2 cups (355 ml) vegetable stock

1 sheet frozen parve puff pastry

Preheat the oven to 400°F (200°C, or gas mark 6). Bring a large saucepan of water to a boil. Add the potatoes and cook for 3 minutes. Add the carrots and squash and cook for 3 minutes. Add the broccoli and cook for 2 minutes. Drain the vegetables and set them aside together. Heat the olive oil in a large sauté pan over medium heat. Add the onion and cook for 2 minutes. Add the garlic and cook briefly. Add the potatoes, carrots, squash, broccoli, and corn; sprinkle with the parsley, thyme, salt, and pepper; and mix to distribute the ingredients evenly. Sprinkle the flour over the ingredients and mix gently. Cook for 2 minutes. Pour in the stock and mix the ingredients. Bring the liquid to a simmer and cook for 3 to 4 minutes or until the liquid is slightly thickened. Spoon the ingredients into a 6-cup (1.4-L) casserole dish. Roll the puff pastry sheet to fit the top of the casserole. Place the pastry over the vegetables. Bake for about 20 minutes or until the top is golden brown and puffed.

Yield: Makes 4 servings

SERVING SUGGESTIONS AND VARIATIONS: You can make this in individual baking dishes instead of one large casserole dish. If you don't want to use potatoes, substitute cut-up cauliflower or parsnips.

FISH

With so many nutritional benefits, fish has become a must for all home cooks. But fish has even more plusses: You can cook it relatively quickly and without much fuss. And, because many varieties are available to choose from, it is extraordinarily versatile. For kosher cooks, there's one more bonus: Fish is parve, so it can be eaten with either meat or dairy ingredients. But note that some Jewish groups do not eat fish together with dairy or fish together with meat.

SEARED COD WITH PAN SALSA

(P)

Crispy-crusted fish is so attractive that even this everyday main course looks special and welcoming.

4 cod fillets, about 6 ounces (170 g) each, skin intact

1/4 cup (32 g) all-purpose flour

Salt and freshly ground black pepper, to taste

3 tablespoons (45 ml) vegetable oil, divided

1 medium onion, chopped

2 stalks celery, sliced about 1/4 inch (6 mm) thick

1 large clove garlic, chopped

3 dozen halved grape tomatoes

2 tablespoons (5 g) chopped fresh basil

2 tablespoons (30 ml) lemon juice

TIP

You can make this with skinless fish but the skin holds the fillets together better.

Preheat the oven to warm. Pat the fish dry with paper towels. Mix the flour, salt, and pepper together in a dish. Coat the fish with the flour mixture. Heat 2 tablespoons (30 ml) of the vegetable oil in a large sauté pan over medium-high heat. Place the fish, skin side down, in the pan and cook for about 5 minutes. Carefully turn the fish over and cook for another 4 to 5 minutes or until cooked through. Place the fillets on a serving platter and keep warm in the oven.

Pour the remaining tablespoon (15 ml) vegetable oil in the pan. Lower the heat to medium. Add the onion and celery and cook, stirring frequently, for about 3 minutes or until the vegetables have softened. Add the garlic and cook briefly. Add the tomatoes and basil and cook for another 1 to 2 minutes. Sprinkle with the lemon juice and freshly ground black pepper to taste. Spoon the vegetables alongside the fish and serve.

Yield: Makes 4 servings

ROASTED SALMON WITH LEMON, ROSEMARY, AND HAZELNUTS

(P)

This is a good dish when you're in a hurry. It takes less than 15 minutes to prepare and about 15 minutes to cook, making it a terrific weekday choice. Add cooked noodles, sautéed sugar snap peas, or spinach for a colorful, filling meal that takes less than a half hour.

4 salmon fillets or steaks, 6 to 8 ounces (170 to 225 g) each, about 1¼ inches (3 cm) thick
3 tablespoons (45 ml) lemon juice
2 tablespoons (30 ml) olive oil
1 teaspoon Dijon mustard
1 clove garlic, finely chopped
2 teaspoons (1.5 g) chopped fresh rosemary
1 teaspoon grated fresh lemon peel
1 teaspoon ground coriander
2 tablespoons (47 g) ground hazelnuts
Salt and freshly ground black pepper, to taste

Preheat the oven to 475°F (240°C, or gas mark 9). Place the salmon in a baking dish. In a small bowl, combine the lemon juice, olive oil, mustard, garlic, rosemary, lemon peel, and coriander. Spoon equal amounts of this mixture over each fish. Sprinkle with the hazelnuts and salt and pepper. Roast for about 15 minutes, depending on thickness, or until cooked to desired doneness.

Yield: Makes 4 servings

GRILLED HALIBUT WITH HOT AND SPICY MARINATED PINEAPPLE

(P)

A thick hunk of halibut is one of my favorites to grill because it's so meaty. It is also mild, making it the perfect foil for highly seasoned side dishes such as hot and spicy marinated pineapple.

For the Hot and Spicy Marinated Pineapple:

1 whole pineapple

3 tablespoons (60 g) honey

2 tablespoons (30 ml) vegetable oil

1 tablespoon (15 g) sriracha

2 tablespoons (30 ml) lime juice

Kosher salt or Maldon sea salt

Mint, for garnish

For the Grilled Halibut:

4 halibut fillets or steaks, 6 to 8 ounces (170 to 225 g) each

2 tablespoons (30 ml) olive oil

Salt and freshly ground black pepper, to taste

Make the Hot and Spicy Marinated Pineapple: Cut the leaves off the pineapple. Remove the outer fibrous rind. Cut the peeled pineapple in slices about 3/4-inch (1.9-cm) thick. Set aside in a single layer in a pan. Heat the honey with the vegetable oil and sriracha in a saucepan over medium heat, stirring until the ingredients are well mixed. Add the lime juice. Pour over the pineapple slices. Coat the pineapple slices on both sides and let marinate for at least 1 hour (and as long as 12 hours). Preheat an outdoor grill to medium (or use a grill pan or the oven broiler). Grill the slices for about 4 minutes per side or until well glazed and tender, brushing occasionally with some of the honey mixture. Serve sprinkled lightly with salt. Garnish with fresh mint. You can make these ahead and refrigerate. Serve at room temperature or reheat to warm in a preheated 350°F (180°C, or gas mark 4) oven for a few minutes. Makes 4 to 6 servings.

Make the Grilled Halibut: Prepare the pineapple and set it aside. Preheat an outdoor grill or grill pan over medium heat. Coat the fish with the olive oil and sprinkle with salt and pepper. Cook the fish (cover the grill or pan) for 4 to 5 minutes per side or until cooked through. Serve with Hot and Spicy Marinated Pineapple.

Yield: Makes 4 servings

SERVING SUGGESTIONS AND VARIATIONS: Grilled, spiced pineapple lends monumental flavor to mild main-course foods such as fish and chicken.

FISH CURRY WITH STAR ANISE, CHILE PEPPER, AND COCONUT MILK

(P)

Many years ago I was lucky enough to travel to Malaysia. The place is thrilling for many reasons, but it's the food that lingers most in my memory. Most of the dishes I tasted were hot and spicy but also complex and sophisticated. I still love this kind of cooking with its mix of heat and fragrance, chile peppers balanced with warm spices such as cinnamon, ginger, and star anise.

2 pounds (455 g) tilapia or snapper

2 tablespoons (30 ml) vegetable oil

1 onion or 2 large shallots, chopped

1 medium carrot, diced

2 large cloves garlic, chopped

2 teaspoons chopped fresh ginger

1 medium jalapeño pepper, deseeded and chopped

1 tablespoon (3 g) curry powder

1 cinnamon stick, about 3 inches (7.5-cm) long

2 star anise

2 cups (475 ml) coconut milk

3 tablespoons (45 ml) lemon juice

Salt, to taste

Steamed rice, for serving

Cut the fish into pieces about 2 inches (5 cm) square and set aside. Heat the vegetable oil in a large sauté pan over medium heat. Add the shallots and carrot and cook for 2 to 3 minutes, or until softened. Add the garlic, ginger, and jalapeño pepper and cook for 1 minute. Sprinkle in the curry powder and stir it into the vegetables. Add the cinnamon stick and star anise to the pan. Pour in the coconut milk and lemon juice and stir the ingredients. Bring the mixture to a boil, lower the heat to a simmer, and cook for 4 to 5 minutes or until the liquid has thickened slightly. Immerse the fish in the sauce. Cover the pan and cook for 4 minutes. Remove the cover and cook for another 4 minutes or until the fish is cooked through. Season to taste with salt. Serve over steamed rice.

Yield: Makes 4 servings

SERVING SUGGESTIONS AND VARIATIONS: You can make this into a vegetarian dish by substituting extra firm tofu for the fish (use 2 cups [500 g] of 1-inch [2.5-cm] cubes).

ROASTED SALMON WITH DUKKAH, GARLIC, ORANGE, AND MINT

(P)

We eat salmon so often that finding new seasonings and flavorings is a must. Dukkah, beloved and traditional in Egypt, is a blend of nuts, seeds, and spices. The recipe is incredibly flexible and useful. It does wonders for salmon!

For the Dukkah:

1/4 cup (31 g) shelled roasted pistachios

1/4 cup (34 g) whole roasted hazelnuts

1/4 cup (36 g) sesame seeds

2 tablespoons (12 g) ground coriander

1 1/2 teaspoons ground cumin

1 teaspoon kosher salt

1/2 teaspoon paprika

1/4 teaspoon freshly ground black pepper

For the Roasted Salmon:

4 salmon fillets (6 ounces, or 170 g each)

1 tablespoon (15 ml) olive oil

1 tablespoon (15 ml) lemon juice

1 medium clove garlic, finely chopped

2 teaspoons grated fresh orange peel

1 tablespoon (6 g) chopped fresh mint

1 1/2 tablespoons (11 g) Dukkah

Salt, to taste

Make the Dukkah: Place the pistachios and hazelnuts in an unoiled pan and cook over medium heat, shaking the pan occasionally, for 2 to 3 minutes. Add the sesame seeds and cook for another 2 to 3 minutes or until the ingredients are lightly toasted. Remove the pan from the heat and set aside to cool. Place the mixture in a food processor or spice grinder and process until finely chopped. Mix in the coriander, cumin, salt, paprika, and pepper. Makes just under 1 cup (124 g).

TIP

Keep Dukkah in the refrigerator because nuts can become rancid quickly.

Make the Roasted Salmon: Preheat the oven to 450°F (230°C, or gas mark 8). Place the fish inside a roasting pan. Combine the olive oil, lemon juice, garlic, orange peel, mint, and Dukkah in a bowl and spread on top of the fish. Sprinkle with salt to taste. Roast for about 15 minutes or until cooked through to degree of doneness desired.

Yield: Makes 4 servings

TILAPIA WITH CHORIZO CRUMBS (M)

Baked fish is one of the easiest dinner entrées: Sprinkle the fish with olive oil, herbs, and a few bread crumbs, then bake it and you're done! If it's mild fish such as tilapia, it's also easy to jazz it up with robust ingredients. I've used chile peppers, lemongrass, and capers, but I especially love a flourish of spicy chorizo.

1 cup (60 g) packed fresh bread crumbs

1 kosher chorizo sausage, finely chopped

3 tablespoons (11 g) chopped fresh parsley

2 scallions, chopped

1/4 cup (60 ml) olive oil

4 tilapia fillets, about 6 ounces (170 g) each

Preheat the oven to 400°F (200°C, or gas mark 6). Combine the bread crumbs, chorizo, parsley, and scallions in a bowl, pour in the olive oil, and mix to coat the ingredients evenly. Place the fish in a single layer in a baking pan. Crumble the bread-crumb mixture on top. Bake for about 15 minutes or until the crust is golden brown and the fish is cooked through.

Yield: Makes 4 servings

CAJUN FRIED FISH SANDWICH WITH LIME-PICKLE MAYO

(P)

Fried food is one of our favorites. I mean fried anything. I like to serve this dish on a Sunday when we're just hanging out and a sandwich is sufficient for dinner.

For the Lime-Pickle Mayo:

1/2 cup (115 g) mayonnaise

2 tablespoons (18 g) chopped sweet pickle

1½ tablespoons (22.5 ml) lime juice

2 teaspoons (4 g) grated lime peel

For the Fish Sandwich:

4 white fish fillets (such as flounder, sole, etc.)

1/2 cup (120 ml) coconut or soy milk

2/3 cup (83.5 g) all-purpose flour

2 large eggs

2 teaspoons (10 ml) water

1 cup (145 g) cornmeal

1 teaspoon salt, or to taste

1/2 teaspoon cayenne pepper

1½ teaspoons finely chopped fresh thyme (or 1/2 teaspoon dried)

1/4 teaspoon garlic powder

Vegetable oil

8 slices bread (toast, baguette, etc.)

Lettuce and tomato slices

Make the Lime-Pickle Mayo: Mix the mayonnaise, pickle, lime juice, and lime peel together until well mixed. Makes about 2/3 cup (180 g).

Make the Fish Sandwich: Place the fillets in a shallow dish and pour the milk over them. Let soak for about 15 minutes, turning at least once. Place the flour on a plate. In a bowl, beat the eggs and water together. On another plate, combine the cornmeal, salt, cayenne pepper, thyme, and garlic powder. Dredge each fillet in the flour and shake off the excess. Coat the floured fish with the egg and then the cornmeal mixture. Place the fillets on a plate or cake rack and air-dry for 15 to 20 minutes. Heat about 1/4 inch (6 mm) vegetable oil in a sauté pan over medium-high heat. When the oil is hot, add the fillets, and cook for about 2 minutes per side or until they are golden brown. Drain on paper towels. Place 2 bread slices on each of 4 plates. Place lettuce and 1 to 2 tomato slices on top of one bread slice per plate. Top with one fillet. Pour equal amounts of Lime-Pickle Mayo over the fish. Top with the second bread slice.

Yield: Makes 4 servings

HALIBUT CHOWDER

(P)

When I don't feel like fussing with a main course, sometimes soup is supper. This chowder is filling enough for that. I serve it with ciabatta (good to dunk into the soup) or another hearty bread.

2 tablespoons (30 ml) olive oil

1 medium onion, chopped

1 red bell pepper, deseeded and chopped

1 small chile pepper, deseeded and minced

1 large garlic clove, finely chopped

3 tablespoons (48 g) tomato paste

1 can (28 ounces, or 794 g) tomatoes, coarsely chopped, including juices

4 cups (950 ml) vegetable or fish stock

1 cup (235 ml) white wine

2 tablespoons (5 g) chopped fresh basil

2 tablespoons (7.5 g) chopped fresh parsley

3 medium carrots, diced (about 1/4-inch, or 6 mm)

1 medium zucchini, diced (about 1/4-inch, or 6 mm)

1 1/2 pounds (680 g) halibut, cut into chunks

Salt and freshly ground black pepper, to taste

Heat the olive oil in a large sauté pan over medium heat. Add the onion, bell pepper, and chile pepper and cook for 2 to 3 minutes or until softened slightly. Add the garlic and cook briefly. Stir in the tomato paste. Add the tomatoes, stock, white wine, basil, and parsley. Bring to a simmer, cover the pan partially, and cook for 20 minutes.

Add the carrots and zucchini, cover the pan partially, and cook for another 10 minutes. Add the halibut. Season with salt and pepper to taste, cover the pan, and cook for 8 to 10 minutes or until the fish is cooked through.

Yield: Makes 4 servings

SERVING SUGGESTIONS AND VARIATIONS: You can add all sorts of ingredients to this dish: cooked rice or egg noodles and vegetables such as corn, peas, or chopped green string beans. I have used several varieties of fish, too, including cod, haddock, and perch.

PANKO-COCONUT-CRUSTED ARCTIC CHAR WITH ARUGULA-SCALLION BUTTER

(D)

Arctic char is a relative of both salmon and trout, and I think it has the best features of each. It's soft and sweet like trout, flavorful but not as bold as salmon. Like salmon, it's a good source of omega-3 fatty acids. You can fry it, like trout; you can roast or grill it, like salmon. In this recipe I like how the sweet coconut-y crust and the bitter arugula leaves complement the mild fish flavor.

1/2 cup (10 g) arugula leaves

5 tablespoons (70 g) softened butter

1 scallion, chopped

1 teaspoon finely chopped lime peel

2 teaspoons lime juice

1/4 cup (32 g) all-purpose flour

1 large egg

2 teaspoons water

3/4 cup (37.5 g) panko

1/2 cup (43 g) finely grated unsweetened coconut

4 Arctic char fillets (6 ounces, or 170 g, each)

Salt, to taste

Preheat the oven to 500°F (250°C, or gas mark 10). Chop the arugula and place it in a food processor. Add the butter, scallion, lime peel and juice and process until well blended. Set aside. Place the flour in a dish. Mix the egg and water in a second dish. Mix the panko and coconut and place it in a third dish. Dredge each fillet in the flour and shake off the excess. Coat the floured fish with the egg. Coat the fillets with the panko mixture. Sprinkle with salt to taste. Place the fillets in a roasting pan and roast for 13 to 15 minutes or until lightly browned and cooked through. Serve each fillet with some of the arugula-scallion butter.

Yield: Makes 4 servings

SERVING SUGGESTIONS AND VARIATIONS: You can fry the fish instead of roasting it. After coating the fillets, place them on a plate or cake rack and let them rest 15 to 20 minutes. Heat about 1/4 inch (6 mm) of vegetable oil in a sauté pan over medium-high heat. When the oil is hot, add the fillets, and cook them for 2 to 3 minutes per side or until they are cooked through and golden brown on both sides. Drain the fish on paper towels.

BAKED FISH WITH VEGETABLES, HERBS, AND SPICES

(P)

This is a beautiful one-pot fish dish. It's magically fragrant as it cooks and although it's well-seasoned, it's not overly spicy. I set it up hours ahead so it's ready to bake when I need to get dinner together. You may find branzini sold under the name European sea bass.

1 red bell pepper, deseeded and cut into small chunks

1 medium jalapeño pepper, deseeded and chopped

4 whole branzini, gutted

2 tomatoes, cut into chunks

1 medium zucchini, cut into bite-size pieces

1/4 cup (15 g) chopped fresh parsley

2 tablespoons (5 g) chopped fresh basil

2 large cloves garlic, finely chopped

1/2 teaspoon ground coriander

1/2 teaspoon paprika

1/2 teaspoon ground cumin

2 tablespoons (30 ml) olive oil

2 tablespoons (30 ml) lemon juice

Salt, to taste

Place the red pepper and jalapeño inside a large, lightly oiled baking dish. Place the branzini on top. Scatter the tomatoes and zucchini around the fish. In a small bowl, combine the parsley, basil, garlic, coriander, paprika, cumin, olive oil, and lemon juice. Brush this mixture on the fish and vegetables. Sprinkle with salt. Let marinate for at least 1 hour.

Preheat the oven to 325°F (170°C, or gas mark 3). Cover the dish and bake for 20 minutes. Raise the oven heat to 400°F (200°C, or gas mark 6). Remove the cover and bake for another 10 minutes.

Yield: Makes 4 servings

SERVING SUGGESTIONS AND VARIATIONS: You can use any similar fish such as red snapper, whiting, or thick fillets of cod or halibut. You can also use richer fish such as pompano.

chapter
····················

MEAT

Because so many kosher meat cuts come from muscular, sinewy parts of the animal, we typically use them for pot roast and stew, those long, slow-cooking methods that break down the tough fibers. But meat lovers won't be put off by the hunky chew of quickly cooked Grilled Korean-Style Short Ribs made with old-fashioned flanken. And because meat is salted and soaked to conform to the dietary laws, it can be salty—making it unhealthy for some. But by using fresh herbs, chile peppers, chutney, unusual condiments, fresh and dried fruits, and vegetables and other ingredients that enhance flavor, you can go easy on the salt. With a dish such as the Grilled Veal Chops with Meyer Lemon Chutney, you might not need to add any salt.

GRILLED KOREAN-STYLE SHORT RIBS   Ⓜ

My grandma made flanken, but not like this! She cooked it for hours, in soup or stew. And that's the way most people cook this cut (a.k.a. short ribs) because it can be tough and chewy when you grill it quickly. But for the carnivores among us (that would include Ed and me), this meaty chewiness is actually incredibly satisfying. And short ribs are bountiful with beef flavor.

1/4 cup (60 ml) soy sauce

2 tablespoons (40 g) honey

2 tablespoons (30 ml) mirin

1 tablespoon (15 ml) vegetable oil

1 tablespoon (15 ml) sesame seed oil

3 scallions, finely chopped

2 cloves garlic, finely chopped

2 teaspoons (4 g) finely chopped fresh ginger

1 tablespoon (8 g) toasted sesame seeds, finely crushed

1 teaspoon crushed red pepper

3 pounds (1.4 kg) flanken

Place the soy sauce, honey, mirin, vegetable oil, sesame seed oil, scallions, garlic, ginger, sesame seeds, and crushed red pepper in a bowl and stir until the ingredients are well combined. Place the beef in a nonreactive dish and pour the soy sauce mixture on top. Turn the pieces to coat them on all sides. Let marinate in the refrigerator for at least 1 hour, turning the pieces once or twice during that time.

Preheat the oven broiler, outdoor grill, or grill pan and grill the meat for 3 to 4 minutes per side or until crispy.

Yield: Makes 4 to 6 servings

GRILLED SKIRT STEAK WITH PONZU MARINADE

Ⓜ

Ponzu is one of those magical mixtures, so versatile you'll wonder how you ever cooked without it. You can buy bottled versions, but you can quickly and easily make it fresh, from scratch, at home—and doing so is well worth the time and effort. Fresh citrus gives ponzu a richer, more refreshing taste than something that's built for shelf life.

For the Ponzu Sauce:

/2 cup (120 ml) orange juice

/4 cup (60 ml) lemon juice

/4 cup (60 ml) lime juice

/2 cup (120 ml) soy sauce

2 tablespoons (30 ml) rice vinegar

2 tablespoons (30 ml) mirin

2 medium cloves garlic, finely chopped

1 tablespoon (6 g) fresh ginger, grated

1 teaspoon finely chopped chile pepper

2 scallions, finely chopped

2 teaspoons chopped fresh cilantro

For the Steak:

2 pounds (900 g) skirt steak

1/2 cup (120 ml) Ponzu Sauce

Make the Ponzu Sauce: Place the juices, soy sauce, rice vinegar, and mirin in a bowl. Add the garlic, ginger, chile pepper, scallions, and cilantro. Mix well and let rest for 1 hour or more before using. Makes about 13/4 cups (410 ml). Keep Ponzu Sauce in a tightly closed container in the fridge; it will stay fresh testing for about a week.

Make the Steak: Place the steaks in a nonreactive shallow pan. Pour the Ponzu Sauce over the meat, turning the pieces to coat both sides. Place in the refrigerator to marinate for at least 1 hour, turning the meat once or twice during that time. Preheat an outdoor grill, indoor grill pan, or oven broiler. Remove the steaks from the marinade (but reserve the marinade to use during grilling). Grill the steaks for 6 to 8 minutes, or until they are cooked to desired doneness, turning them occasionally and brushing with the Ponzu Sauce.

Yield: Makes 4 servings

SERVING SUGGESTIONS AND VARIATIONS: You can use ponzu as a marinade for chicken and fish and for glazing grilled or roasted vegetables (asparagus are especially tasty with ponzu).

BEEF CHUCK ROAST WITH HORSERADISH MASHED POTATOES

(M)

Here's where fresh herbs help make plain old pot roast into something special. We like it with mashed potatoes, and better yet, when those potatoes include a little horseradish oomph.

For the Pot Roast:

4 pounds (1.8 kg) boneless chuck roast

1/4 cup (32 g) all-purpose flour

Freshly ground black pepper, to taste

4 tablespoons (60 ml) vegetable oil, divided

3 medium onions, quartered

6 carrots, cut into chunks

2 stalks celery, sliced

2 cloves garlic, cut into pieces

1 3/4 cups (410 ml) beef stock

1 cup (235 ml) red wine

3 to 4 sprigs thyme

3 to 4 sprigs fresh rosemary

For the Mashed Potatoes:

4 medium Yukon gold potatoes, peeled

3 tablespoons (45 ml) olive oil

2 tablespoons (45 g) prepared white horseradish

4 to 5 tablespoons (60 to 75 ml) vegetable stock

Salt and freshly ground black pepper, to taste

Make the Pot Roast: Preheat oven to 275°F (140°C, or gas mark 1). Rinse and dry the meat. In a dish, mix the flour with black pepper to taste. Dredge the beef in the flour mixture to coat it on all sides. Set aside. Pour 2 tablespoons (30 ml) vegetable oil in a Dutch oven over medium heat. Add the onions and cook for about 2 minutes. Remove the onions to a dish and set aside. Add the carrots and cook them for 2 to 3 minutes or until lightly browned. Place on the dish with the onions. Add the remaining vegetable oil to the pan. Cook the meat, turning it occasionally, for about 8 minutes, or until lightly browned. Remove the pan from the heat. Add the browned onions, carrots, celery, and garlic to the pan. Pour in the stock and wine. Place the thyme and rosemary sprigs in the pan. Cover and place it in the oven. Cook for 4 1/2 to 5 hours or until tender.

Make the Mashed Potatoes: Cut the potatoes into small chunks. Cook them in lightly salted simmering water for about 10 minutes or until tender. Drain the potatoes and mash them in the pan. Pour in the olive oil and horseradish and continue to mash until the potatoes are smooth. Add 4 tablespoons (60 ml) of the stock and blend it in; add the remaining stock, if desired. Taste for seasoning and add salt and pepper.

Yield: Makes 4 to 6 servings

GRILLED VEAL CHOPS WITH MEYER LEMON CHUTNEY

Ⓜ

Veal can be expensive! Sure, the rib portion is tender, tasty, and juicy, but the much cheaper shoulder chops are just fine, too.

For the Meyer Lemon Chutney:

1 teaspoon mustard seeds

1/2 teaspoon aniseeds

1/2 teaspoon black peppercorns

6 whole cloves

1 cinnamon stick, 2-inches (5-cm) long

1 cup (230 g) chopped Meyer lemon (1/4-inch, or 6-mm, pieces)

8 Medjool dates, quartered

1/2 cup (75 g) dried cherries or raisins

11/4 cups (295 g) orange juice

1/3 cup (80 ml) apple cider vinegar

1 cup (200 g) sugar

2 tablespoons (28 g) chopped crystallized ginger

For the Veal Chops:

4 veal chops, about 1-inch (2.5-cm) thick

2 tablespoons (30 ml) olive oil

1 clove garlic, finely chopped

1 tablespoon (4 g) chopped fresh rosemary

2 teaspoons grated fresh lemon peel

Salt and freshly ground black pepper, to taste

Make the Chutney: Toast the mustard seeds and aniseeds in an unoiled saucepan over medium heat for 1 to 2 minutes or until slightly fragrant. Let cool. Place the seeds, peppercorns, cloves, and cinnamon stick in a small muslin bag (or wrap in cheesecloth) and place in the pan. Add the Meyer lemon, dates, cherries, orange juice, apple cider vinegar, sugar, and ginger. Bring the ingredients to a boil over high heat, stirring often. Reduce the heat and simmer for 35 to 40 minutes or until the chutney thickens. Let cool. Remove the muslin bag. Makes about 21/2 cups (625 g).

Make the Veal Chops: Rub the veal with the olive oil. Sprinkle with the garlic, rosemary, lemon peel, salt, and pepper. Marinate in the refrigerator for about 1 hour. Preheat an outdoor grill, grill pan, or oven broiler. Grill the meat for 3 to 4 minutes per side or until cooked to desired doneness. Serve with the chutney.

Yield: Makes 4 servings

SERVING SUGGESTIONS AND VARIATIONS: If you can't find Meyer lemon, use kumquats, limequats, or blood oranges, or a mixture of these.

LAMBURGERS IN PITA WITH LEMON-TAHINI SAUCE

Our family was never much for ground lamburgers until we ate some with this tangy, lemony sauce, which goes so perfectly with the bold, rich meat taste. This is a good summer dish if you have an outdoor grill, but you can make them anytime using a grill pan and even a regular sauté pan.

For the Lamburgers:

1¼ to 1½ pounds (570 to 680 g) ground lamb

½ cup (25 g) fresh bread crumbs

1 medium onion, chopped

1 large garlic clove, minced

1 large egg

3 tablespoons (11 g) chopped fresh parsley

3 tablespoons (18 g) chopped fresh mint

1½ teaspoons ground cumin

1 teaspoon paprika

⅛ teaspoon ground cinnamon

Olive oil

4 medium pita pockets, warmed

Tomatoes, chopped, optional

For the Lemon-Tahini Sauce:

½ cup (120 g) tahini

⅓ cup (80 ml) lemon juice

¼ cup (60 ml) water

2 tablespoons (30 ml) olive oil

2 cloves garlic, finely chopped

Salt, to taste

Make the Lamburgers: Preheat an outdoor grill, oven broiler, or grill pan. Place the ground lamb, bread crumbs, onion, garlic, egg, parsley, mint, cumin, paprika, and cinnamon together in a bowl and mix gently to combine the ingredients thoroughly. Shape the mixture into 4 patties, 1 inch (2.5 cm) thick. Brush the grids (or the pan) with a film of olive oil. Sear the burgers for 1 minute per side then lower the heat to medium. Cook for another 2 to 3 minutes per side or until cooked through. While the burgers are cooking, mix together the Lemon-Tahini Sauce. Place the burgers inside the pita pockets. Drizzle some Lemon-Tahini Sauce on top; add a few spoonfuls of chopped tomato, if desired.

Make the Lemon-Tahini Sauce: Stir the tahini to blend in any oil that has risen to the top. Mix the tahini and lemon juice together, blending ingredients thoroughly. Add the water, olive oil, garlic, and salt. Blend thoroughly. Makes 1 cup (240 g).

Yield: Makes 4 pita sandwiches

BRAISED SHORT RIBS WITH SQUASH AND DRIED FRUIT

(M)

This is another dish I tend to cook on a cold Sunday, when we can relax at home, take in the fragrance of braising meat, and anticipate a hearty, early dinner before we have to get ready for the week ahead. The squash chunks, dried fruit, balsamic vinegar, and whole cloves give the dish a welcome sweet and savory flavor.

4 pounds (1.8 kg) beef short ribs

1/3 cup (42 g) all-purpose flour

2 tablespoons (30 ml) olive oil

2 onions, coarsely chopped

2 cloves garlic, chopped

1 tablespoon (6 g) chopped fresh ginger

3 tablespoons (45 ml) balsamic vinegar

1 tablespoon (11 g) Dijon mustard

2 cups (475 ml) red wine

Salt and freshly ground black pepper, to taste, optional

1 sprig fresh rosemary

6 whole cloves

3 cups (420 g) cubed butternut squash

16 dried apricot halves

4 dried figs, cut into quarters

Rinse the ribs and pat them dry. Dredge the ribs in the flour, coating all sides. Heat the olive oil in a large sauté pan over medium-high heat. Brown the ribs in batches for 6 to 8 minutes, turning them occasionally, to brown all sides. Remove the ribs to a plate and set aside. Add the onions to the pan and lower the heat to medium; cook, stirring, for 2 to 3 minutes. Add the garlic and ginger and cook for another minute. Mix the balsamic vinegar and mustard, mix them with the wine, and pour the liquid into the pan. Return the ribs to pan. Sprinkle with salt and pepper, if desired. Place the rosemary on top. Scatter the cloves around the pan. Bring the liquid to a simmer and turn the heat to low. Cover the pan and cook for 2 1/2 to 3 hours or until the meat is tender. Add the squash, apricots, and figs to the pan. Cook for another 30 minutes or until the squash is tender. Remove the rosemary sprigs and cloves before serving.

Yield: Makes 4 servings

SERVING SUGGESTIONS AND VARIATIONS: You can substitute different dried fruits for the apricots and figs: cranberries, cherries, raisins, peaches, nectarines, and so on.

BRISKET WITH MANGO-BARBECUE SAUCE

Ⓜ

With so many no-red-meat eaters in my family, I don't make brisket too often, but when I do, I do it up big, using a whole brisket first plus second cut. We prefer it Texas-style: grilled and slathered with barbecue sauce that catches the flames to make those fabulous, blackened "burnt ends."

For the Mango-Barbecue Sauce:

1 large ripe mango

2 tablespoons (30 g) vegetable oil

1 medium onion, chopped

1 large clove garlic, minced

1 tablespoon (6 g) finely grated fresh orange peel

1 teaspoon chopped fresh ginger

1 teaspoon chopped jalapeño pepper

1 cup (240 g) ketchup

1/4 cup (60 ml) orange juice

1/4 cup (85 g) molasses

1 tablespoon (15 ml) soy sauce

1 teaspoon white horseradish

For the Brisket:

1 brisket of beef (6 to 12 pounds, or 2.7 to 5.4 kg)

Salt, pepper, garlic powder, and paprika, to taste

2 to 3 large onions, sliced

Make the Mango-Barbecue Sauce: Peel the mango and purée the flesh in a food processor. Set it aside. Heat the vegetable oil in a saucepan over medium heat. Add the onion and cook for 2 to 3 minutes or until slightly softened. Add the garlic, orange peel, ginger, and jalapeño pepper and cook briefly. Add the mango purée, ketchup, orange juice, molasses, soy sauce, and horseradish. Stir thoroughly to blend the ingredients. Bring to a boil over medium-high heat, stir, and lower the heat; cook, stirring occasionally, for about 15 minutes, or until thickened. Let cool. Makes about 2 1/2 cups (625 g).

Make the Brisket: Preheat the oven to 225°F (107°C). Place the meat in a large roasting pan and sprinkle with salt, pepper, garlic powder, and paprika. Scatter the onion slices on top. Sprinkle with more paprika. Cover the pan tightly. Bake for 7 to 8 hours or overnight (less time for a smaller brisket). Remove the meat and onions. Let the meat cool. Just before serving, preheat an outdoor grill or oven broiler. Slather some of the barbecue sauce over the meat and grill or broil for 12 to 15 minutes, occasionally using more sauce as needed. Slice and serve.

Yield: Makes 8 to 16 servings, depending on brisket size

PAN-SEARED MARINATED HANGER STEAKS WITH PEPPERS AND ONIONS Ⓜ

Hanger steaks have become extremely popular in recent years (you may have noticed how expensive they have become as a result). They aren't as elegant as the even more costly rib steaks, but they are flavorful and just perfect for a casual, bistro-type meal. Serve them with "frites" or corn on the cob as accompaniments.

4 hanger steaks (6 ounces, or 170 g, each)
5 tablespoons (75 ml) olive oil, divided
2 tablespoons (30 ml) white wine vinegar
1 teaspoon finely crushed coriander seeds
1 teaspoon Dijon mustard
2 medium cloves garlic, finely chopped
1/2 teaspoon crushed red pepper
1 small red bell pepper, deseeded and sliced

1 small yellow or orange bell pepper, deseeded and sliced
1 Anaheim or Cubanelle pepper, deseeded and sliced
1 to 2 teaspoons chopped jalapeño pepper
1 large sweet onion, sliced
Salt, to taste

Place the steaks in a nonreactive shallow pan. Combine 3 tablespoons (45 ml) olive oil, the white wine vinegar, coriander seeds, mustard, garlic, and red pepper. Spoon this mixture over the steaks, turning the pieces to coat both sides. Marinate in the refrigerator for at least 1 hour, turning the meat once or twice during that time. Preheat the oven to warm (lowest temperature). Heat the remaining 2 tablespoons (30 ml) olive oil in a large sauté pan over medium heat. Add all the peppers and the onion and sprinkle with salt. Sauté, stirring occasionally, for 8 to 10 minutes, or until the vegetables have softened and are beginning to brown. Spoon the mixture into an ovenproof dish and keep warm in the oven. Turn the heat under the sauté pan to medium-high. Add the steaks and cook for 3 to 5 minutes per side or until cooked to the desired doneness. Place the steaks on top of the peppers (or surround the meat with the peppers) and serve.

Yield: Makes 4 servings

SERVING SUGGESTIONS AND VARIATIONS: You can make this dish with skirt steak. Use any kind of peppers you wish; the ones suggested here add color and a range of tastes from hot to sweet. The sweet onions give a good balance to the peppers, but common yellow onions will do, too.

BRAISED VEAL SHANKS WITH TOMATOES

(M)

This is such a favorite main course that I make a bunch of it on a Sunday and pack portions up for freezing—a real convenience when I have no time to cook an entire dinner. We like this on top of spaghetti, but when I have time, I serve it with polenta.

4 large or 8 small veal shanks, about 2 inches (5 cm) thick

1/4 cup (32 g) flour

3 tablespoons (45 ml) olive oil

2 medium carrots, chopped

1 stalk celery, chopped

1 medium onion, chopped

2 large garlic cloves, chopped

1 strip lemon peel, about 1 inch (2.5 cm) long

1/2 cup (120 ml) beef stock

1/2 cup (120 ml) white wine

1 pound (455 g) plum tomatoes, chopped

2 tablespoons (32 g) tomato paste

Salt and freshly ground black pepper, to taste

3 tablespoons (11 g) chopped fresh parsley

1 teaspoon dried oregano

Dredge the veal shanks in the flour. Shake off excess flour. Heat the olive oil in a deep sauté pan over medium heat. Add the shanks and cook them for 10 to 12 minutes, turning the meat occasionally, until they are browned. Remove the meat from the pan. Add the carrots, celery, onion, and garlic to the pan and cook for 3 to 4 minutes, stirring occasionally. Add the lemon peel, stock, wine, tomatoes, and tomato paste and stir to blend in the tomato paste completely. Bring the ingredients to a simmer. Return the meat to the pan. Sprinkle with the salt, pepper, parsley, and oregano. Cover the pan, turn the heat to a bare simmer, and cook for about 2 hours or until the meat is very tender. Turn the shanks occasionally during cooking time.

Yield: Makes 4 servings

SERVING SUGGESTIONS AND VARIATIONS: This recipe is very flexible. I've made it with red wine and chicken stock, used canned tomatoes, and substituted fresh basil or marjoram for the dried oregano. All good!

POULTRY

Chicken, turkey, duck, and Cornish hens are all poultry. In a way, however, they are chameleons, too—adaptable and flexible beyond compare, changing their character and the way they look and taste depending on the seasoning, accompaniment, or cooking method we use to prepare them. Because kosher poultry is soaked and salted, there's also built-in brining. That means whether you roast, grill, fry, or braise it, the odds are that the meat will always be tender and juicy.

ROASTED CHICKEN BREASTS WITH CITRUS AND HONEY

Ⓜ

We eat chicken more often than any other meat. To keep it from becoming boring, I use different herbs, spices, condiments, basting fluids, and so on to change the taste each time. It takes just a little citrus peel and fresh ginger to give a boost to chicken's mild flavor.

4 large half bone-in chicken breasts	1 large clove garlic, finely chopped
2 tablespoons (30 ml) vegetable oil	1 teaspoon thyme leaves
2 tablespoons (7.5 g) chopped parsley	2 tablespoons (40 g) honey
2 teaspoons finely grated orange peel	1/8 teaspoon cayenne pepper
1 teaspoon finely grated lime peel	Salt and freshly ground black pepper, to taste
1 teaspoon finely chopped fresh ginger	1/3 cup (80 ml) orange juice
2 medium scallions, finely chopped	2 tablespoons (30 ml) lime juice

Rinse and dry the chicken pieces. In a bowl combine the vegetable oil, parsley, orange and lime peels, ginger, scallions, garlic, thyme, honey, and cayenne pepper and mix thoroughly. Season with salt and pepper. Add the chicken to the bowl and coat the pieces with the mixture. Let marinate for at least 1 hour in the refrigerator. Preheat the oven to 425°F (220°C, or gas mark 7). Mix the orange and lime juices together and set aside. Place the chicken, skin side down, in a baking pan. Bake for 10 minutes. Reduce the heat to 350°F (180°C, or gas mark 4). Turn the chicken pieces. Pour the juice over the chicken. Continue to bake for about 30 minutes, basting occasionally with the pan juices or until cooked through (a meat thermometer inserted into the thickest part will read 160°F [71°C]).

Yield: Makes 4 servings

SERVING SUGGESTIONS AND VARIATIONS: You can also make this with 4 whole legs or a whole, cut-up chicken.

SAUTÉED TURKEY CUTLETS WITH ROASTED PINEAPPLE SALSA

(M)

If you've never tasted roasted pineapple, you're in for a treat, because as it cooks it smells like candy and it tastes like a combination of rum and caramel. It works perfectly with simply cooked turkey.

For the Roasted Pineapple Salsa:

1/2 large pineapple, skin removed, cut into slices about 1/2-inch (1.3-cm) thick

1 tablespoon (14 g) coconut oil, melted

Salt, to taste

1 cup (34 g) packed coarsely chopped watercress leaves

1 avocado, peeled and diced

2 scallions, chopped

2 tablespoons (12 g) chopped fresh mint

2 teaspoons chopped chile pepper, optional

2 tablespoons (30 ml) lime juice

1 tablespoon (20 g) honey

For the Turkey Cutlets:

1/2 cup (65 g) all-purpose flour

Salt and cayenne pepper, to taste

1 1/2 to 2 pounds (680 to 900 g) turkey cutlets

Vegetable oil, for frying

Make the Roasted Pineapple Salsa: Preheat the oven to 500°F (250°C, or gas mark 10). Line a cookie sheet with parchment paper. Brush the pineapple slices with the coconut oil. Place the slices on the cookie sheet and sprinkle with salt. Roast for 10 minutes per side or until lightly browned. Remove the slices from the oven and let cool to room temperature. Chop them into bite-size pieces, removing and discarding the hard fibrous core. Place the pineapple pieces in a bowl. Add the watercress leaves, avocado, scallions, mint, chile pepper, if used, lime juice, and honey and toss to distribute the ingredients evenly. Let rest at least 15 minutes before serving on top of the turkey. Makes about 2 1/2 cups (625 g).

Make the Turkey Cutlets: Preheat the oven to the lowest temperature. Mix the flour, salt, and cayenne pepper together on a dish. Dredge the cutlets in the flour mixture and shake off the excess. Heat a small amount of vegetable oil in a sauté pan over medium heat. Add the cutlets a few at a time and cook for about 2 minutes per side or until lightly browned. Place on paper towels on a cookie sheet and keep warm in the oven. Repeat with the remaining cutlets. Serve with the salsa.

Yield: Makes 4 servings

DUCK LEGS WITH SAUSAGE STUFFING (M)

Duck legs are much easier to prepare than a whole duck and take less time, too. And there's no carving to do! Duck is fatty, so it goes well with bread stuffing, which absorbs the fat as it melts in the heat of the oven. The result is a savory, rich side dish with the meat.

1/4 cup (55 g) dried wild mushrooms

3 tablespoons (45 ml) olive oil, divided

1/2 pound (225 g) chicken sausage, chopped into small pieces

1/3 cup (53 g) chopped shallot

1 large clove garlic, chopped

3 tablespoons (27 g) pine nuts

2 tablespoons (7.5 g) chopped fresh parsley

1 1/2 tablespoons (3 g) chopped fresh rosemary

4 cups 1/2-inch (1.3 cm) diced bread cubes

Salt and freshly ground black pepper, to taste

1/2 cup (120 ml) chicken stock

4 whole duck legs

Preheat the oven to 400°F (200°C, or gas mark 6). Place the mushrooms in a small bowl, cover with hot water, and let soak for about 10 minutes or until they are soft. Drain, chop the mushrooms and set them aside in a large bowl. Heat 1 tablespoon (15 ml) of the olive oil in a large sauté pan over medium heat. Add the sausage and cook for 4 to 5 minutes or until the meat has browned. Remove the meat from the pan and place it in the bowl with the mushrooms. Pour 1 tablespoon (15 ml) olive oil into the pan and cook the shallot, garlic, and pine nuts for 2 to 3 minutes, or until lightly toasted. Add them to the bowl with the mushrooms and sausage. Add the parsley, rosemary, bread cubes, salt, and pepper. Pour in the chicken stock. Toss to distribute the ingredients evenly. Place the stuffing inside a roasting pan. Rinse and dry the duck legs. Remove any excess fat. Rub the legs with the remaining tablespoon (15 ml) olive oil. Sprinkle with salt and pepper to taste. Cook them over medium heat in the pan used for the sausage, for 3 to 5 minutes per side, or until nicely browned. Place the legs, skin side down, on top of the stuffing in the roasting pan. Roast for 30 minutes. Turn the legs skin side up. Roast for another 30 minutes or until cooked through and lightly crispy and browned.

Yield: Makes 4 servings

SERVING SUGGESTIONS AND VARIATIONS: You can use the same stuffing for a whole duck, or to fill 12 quail, or 6 Cornish hens. Cranberry sauce and sautéed spinach, chard, watercress, or lightly sautéed mesclun would be tasty accompaniments.

ROASTED CHICKEN WITH BAHARAT, GARLIC, AND MINT

(M)

Baharat is an intriguing spice mixture popular in the Middle East. The typical blends include cinnamon, nutmeg, cumin, and coriander, and sometimes cayenne pepper and dried mint. My formula is mildly spicy and quick and easy to mix. Baharat is perfect with mild foods such as chicken and roasted vegetables and on vegetable soup.

For the Baharat:

1 tablespoon (6 g) ground coriander

1 tablespoon (5.5 g) ground ginger

2 teaspoons ground cinnamon

1 teaspoon each ground allspice, ground cumin, and freshly ground black pepper

1/2 teaspoon each freshly grated nutmeg, ground cardamom, cayenne pepper, and paprika

For the Roasted Chicken:

1 roasting chicken, 4 to 6 pounds (1.8 to 2.7 kg)

21/2 tablespoons (37.5 ml) olive oil, divided

Salt, to taste

2 large cloves garlic, finely chopped

2 tablespoons (12 g) finely chopped fresh mint

1 teaspoon finely grated lemon peel

2 teaspoons Baharat

3/4 cup (175 ml) chicken stock

Make the Baharat: Mix all the Baharat ingredients together until thoroughly blended. Store in an airtight container in a cabinet. Makes about 1/4 cup (25 g).

Make the Roasted Chicken: Preheat the oven to 500°F (250°C, or gas mark 10). Remove any pin-feathers and extra flesh and fat from the chicken. Take out the package of giblets inside the cavity (you may save these pieces for stock, except for the liver, or roast them along with the chicken). Rinse and dry the chicken. Rub with 1/2 tablespoon olive oil and sprinkle with salt. Place the chicken, breast side down, on a rack in a roasting pan. Roast for 10 minutes. Combine the remaining olive oil, garlic, mint, lemon peel, and Baharat in a bowl. Brush the chicken with half of the spice mixture. Lower the oven heat to 350°F (180°C, or gas mark 4). Roast for another 10 minutes and pour the chicken stock over the chicken. Roast for another 20 minutes. Baste the chicken and turn it, breast-side up. Brush the chicken with the remaining spice mixture. Roast for 45 to 60 minutes, basting occasionally with the pan juices, or until cooked through (a meat thermometer inserted into the thickest part of the breast will register 160°F [71°C]). Let rest for 15 minutes before carving.

Yield: Makes 4 to 6 servings

ROASTED TURKEY HALF-BREAST WITH HERBS AND VEGETABLES

(M)

Years ago turkey was a once- or twice-a-year dish, but after cut-up parts became available all the time, it became a regular dinner item. I make a turkey half-breast once a week, using different herbs and spices, depending on my mood. This recipe includes vegetables, so it's a meal-in-one, though I usually also serve it with cooked rice.

1 turkey half breast, 3 to 4 pounds (1.4 to 1.8 kg)

2 tablespoons (30 ml) olive oil, divided

1 tablespoon (11 g) Dijon mustard

2 teaspoons chopped fresh rosemary

2 teaspoons fresh thyme leaves

Salt and freshly ground black pepper, to taste

2 to 3 carrots, peeled

2 to 3 parsnips, peeled

1 cup (235 ml) chicken stock

1/3 cup (80 ml) white wine

TIP

I serve the pan fluids separately, as is, but you can boil the juices down for thicker sauce or use it to make traditional gravy thickened with flour.

Preheat the oven to 425°F (220°C, or gas mark 7). Rinse and dry the turkey breast and place it, skin-side up, in a roasting pan. Mix 1 tablespoon (15 ml) olive oil and the mustard together and brush the mixture on the turkey. Sprinkle with the rosemary, thyme, salt, and pepper. Cut the carrots and parsnips into julienne strips and place them in the pan around the turkey. Pour the remaining olive oil over the vegetables and toss to coat them completely. Place the pan in the oven and reduce the heat to 350°F (180°C, or gas mark 4). Roast for 20 minutes. Mix the stock and wine and pour over the turkey and vegetables. Continue to roast for another 20 minutes. Baste the turkey and vegetables with the pan juices. Continue to roast the turkey for another 30 to 45 minutes or until a meat thermometer placed in the thickest part of the breast measures 160°F (71°C), basting occasionally with the pan juices. Remove the turkey from the oven and let rest for about 15 minutes before carving. Serve with the vegetables and pan fluids.

Yield: Makes 4 to 6 servings

PANKO-CRUSTED TURKEY CUTLETS WITH CRANBERRY AND PEAR CHUTNEY

(M)

Our family loves Thanksgiving, and sometimes we have a second holiday dinner in the spring. But when a whole huge turkey just doesn't seem right and we are yearning for that turkey-cranberry sauce combo, these cutlets and chutney do beautifully.

For the Chutney:

12 ounces (340 g) fresh cranberries

1 cup (150 g) brown sugar

2 firm pears, peeled and cut into bite-size chunks

3/4 cup (100 g) raisins

1 cup (235 ml) apple cider

6 tablespoons (90 ml) apple cider vinegar

2 tablespoons (12 g) finely chopped fresh ginger

2 teaspoons chopped chile pepper

For the Turkey Cutlets:

1/2 cup (64 g) all-purpose flour

1 large egg

1 tablespoon (15 ml) water

1 1/2 cups (75 g) Panko breadcrumbs

1/2 teaspoon garlic powder

Salt and freshly ground black pepper, to taste

1 1/2 pounds (680 g) turkey cutlets

Vegetable oil, for frying

Make the Chutney: Place all the chutney ingredients in a saucepan. Mix and bring to a boil over high heat. Reduce the heat and simmer for about 40 minutes or until the sauce has thickened. Let cool. Serve with the turkey cutlets. Makes about 3 cups (750 g).

Make the Turkey Cutlets: Place the flour in a dish. Beat the egg and water in a bowl. Mix the Panko with the garlic powder, salt, and pepper in a third dish. Coat the turkey cutlets with the flour; shake off the excess. Coat the cutlets with the beaten egg. Press the cutlets into the Panko mixture, coating the entire surface. Let the cutlets air-dry for about 15 minutes. Heat about 1/8 inch (3 mm) vegetable oil in a large sauté pan over medium heat. When the oil is hot enough for a Panko crumb to sizzle, add the cutlets, a few at a time, and cook them for 2 to 3 minutes per side or until crispy and cooked through. Drain on paper towels. Serve the cutlets with the chutney.

Yield: Makes 4 servings

DID YOU KNOW? Air-drying helps the coating stick better, so fried foods will become tantalizingly crispy, and you won't wind up with an enormous amount of crumbs in the frying pan.

BAKED CHICKEN THIGHS WITH HOISIN-CHILI BARBECUE SAUCE

(M)

This dish is lightly sweet and tangy. It goes nicely with steamed rice and sautéed baby bok choy.

2 tablespoons (30 ml) vegetable oil

2 scallions, finely chopped

2 large cloves garlic, chopped

1 tablespoon (6 g) chopped fresh ginger

1/2 cup (125 g) hoisin sauce

1/4 cup (70 g) bottled chili sauce

1/4 cup (60 ml) rice vinegar

3 tablespoons (45 g) brown sugar

2 tablespoons (30 ml) soy sauce

1 tablespoon (15 ml) sesame seed oil

1/4 teaspoon 5-spice powder

8 chicken thighs

Heat the vegetable oil in a saucepan over medium heat. Add the scallions, garlic, and ginger and cook for 2 to 3 minutes or until the vegetables have softened. Stir in the hoisin sauce, chili sauce, rice vinegar, brown sugar, soy sauce, sesame seed oil, and 5-spice powder. Stir to blend ingredients. Bring to a simmer over medium heat and cook for 4 to 5 minutes or until slightly thickened. Remove from the heat and let cool.

Place the chicken pieces in a deep dish or plastic container. Pour the cooled barbecue sauce over the chicken and toss to coat all the pieces. Cover the dish and marinate for at least 4 hours.

Preheat the oven to 375°F (190°C, or gas mark 5). Remove the chicken from the sauce and place the pieces in a single layer in a baking pan. Bake for about 30 to 40 minutes or until cooked through, occasionally turning the pieces and brushing with some of the sauce. For a crispier surface, place the chicken under the broiler for 2 to 3 minutes after baking.

Yield: Makes 4 servings

SERVING SUGGESTIONS AND VARIATIONS: Use 4 bone-in chicken breast halves, 4 whole chicken legs, or a whole cut-up chicken.

BRAISED CHICKEN WITH TANGERINE JUICE AND BALSAMIC VINEGAR

(M)

This is an easy dish I cook during the week because it doesn't take much preparation. My daughters say—and I must agree—it is another riff on old-fashioned chicken fricassee (they don't like the name "fricassee"). Whatever you want to call it, though, the tender chicken and gravy is a comfort, especially alongside mashed potatoes or egg noodles.

1 cut-up chicken, about 3 to 4 pounds (1.4 to 1.8 kg)

3 tablespoons (45 ml) vegetable oil, divided

1 medium onion, sliced

1/2 cup (120 ml) tangerine juice

1/2 cup (120 ml) chicken stock

1/4 cup (60 ml) balsamic vinegar

1 teaspoon grated fresh tangerine peel

1 teaspoon fresh thyme leaves

Salt and freshly ground black pepper, to taste

Rinse and dry the chicken and set the pieces aside. Heat 2 tablespoons (30 ml) vegetable oil in a sauté pan over medium heat. Cook the chicken a few pieces at a time for about 8 minutes or until lightly browned, turning the pieces occasionally. Remove the chicken to a dish. Add the remaining tablespoon (15 ml) vegetable oil to the pan. Add the onion and cook for about 2 minutes. Return the chicken and any accumulated juices to the pan. Mix the juice, stock, balsamic vinegar, tangerine peel, and thyme leaves and pour over the chicken. Sprinkle with salt and pepper. Cover the pan and cook for 25 to 30 minutes or until the chicken is cooked through. Remove the chicken to a serving platter. Using a slotted spoon, remove the onions from the pan fluids and spoon them over the chicken. Place the pan over high heat and boil the pan juices for 2 to 3 minutes or until slightly thickened. Pour over the chicken or serve separately.

Yield: Makes 4 servings

SERVING SUGGESTIONS AND VARIATIONS: Tangerine juice is rich and packs a lot of flavor into this dish, but you can use orange juice instead.

ROASTED CORNISH HENS WITH CRANBERRIES AND PEARS

What a beautiful main course this is! I serve the hens with mashed sweet potatoes and sautéed spinach all on one large serving platter. The colors are glorious: golden brown birds with lots of bright red, green, and orange highlights. It's perfect for company or a holiday dinner.

2 large Rock Cornish hens (about 1½ pounds, or 680 g, each)

1 tablespoon (15 ml) vegetable oil

Salt and freshly ground black pepper, to taste

1 teaspoon ras el hanout

1 cup (236 ml) mango juice or apricot nectar

1½ cups (150 g) fresh cranberries

2 large pears, peeled, cored, and quartered

Preheat the oven to 350°F (180°C, or gas mark 4). Rinse and dry the hens. Rub the skin with the vegetable oil and sprinkle with salt, pepper, and ras el hanout. Place the hens, breast side down, on a rack in a roasting pan. Place the pan in the oven and roast for 20 minutes. Pour the juice over the hens. Roast for another 15 minutes; baste and turn the hens, breast side up. Raise the heat to 425°F (220°C, or gas mark 7). Add the cranberries to the pan. Roast for 10 minutes and add the pear quarters to the pan. Baste the ingredients and roast for another 5 to 10 minutes or until the hens are cooked through and the skin is crispy. Cut the hens in half for serving. Place them on a platter, surrounded by the pears and cranberries. Spoon the pan juices on top.

Yield: Makes 4 servings

DID YOU KNOW? Ras el hanout is a Middle Eastern spice blend. Commercial kosher brands are available. You can find a recipe for this seasoning in my first kosher cookbook, *Hip Kosher*.

TURKEY BURGERS WITH CRANBERRY KETCHUP

Ⓜ

Ground turkey makes terrific burgers, but the meat is much milder and much leaner than beef. I add lots of energizing seasonings (sage and orange peel here) and a moisturizing ingredient of some sort (egg and chili sauce here) to keep the burgers juicy.

For the Cranberry Ketchup:

1 tablespoon (15 ml) vegetable oil

3 tablespoons (30 g) grated onion

1 small clove garlic, chopped

2 cups (200 g) fresh cranberries

1/3 cup (50 g) brown sugar

1 tablespoon (11 g) Dijon mustard

1/4 cup (60 ml) orange juice

2 teaspoons soy sauce

For the Burgers:

20 ounces (560 g) ground turkey

1/2 cup (60 g) dry bread crumbs

1 large egg

3 tablespoons (60 g) bottled chili sauce

2 tablespoons (20 g) finely chopped onion

11/2 teaspoons finely chopped fresh sage

1 teaspoon grated fresh orange peel

Salt, to taste

Vegetable oil, for frying

Make the Cranberry Ketchup: Heat the vegetable oil in a saucepan over medium heat. Add the onion and garlic, and cook briefly. Add the cranberries, brown sugar, mustard, orange juice, and soy sauce and stir to mix the ingredients. Bring to a boil over medium heat, whisking the ingredients. Lower the heat to a simmer and cook for about 12 to 15 minutes, mixing the ingredients occasionally, until very thick. Purée the mixture in a blender or with a hand blender. Makes about 11/4 cups (300 g).

Make the Turkey Burgers: Combine the turkey, bread crumbs, egg, chili sauce, onion, sage, orange peel, and salt. Shape the mixture into 4 patties about an inch (2.5 cm) thick. Heat a small amount of vegetable oil in a large sauté pan over medium heat. Cook the burgers for 4 to 5 minutes per side, or until cooked through. Serve with Cranberry Ketchup.

Yield: Makes 4 servings

DID YOU KNOW? Ketchup wasn't always made with tomatoes. It was originally made with fish. As time went on, ketchups were made with mushrooms and then other vegetables. The tomatoey versions came later and were thick and sweet. These versions became such favorites that other kinds of ketchup all but disappeared.

VEGETABLES AND SIDE DISHES

When it comes to vegetables, we tend to focus on their being healthful and nutritious, something we should eat. But vegetables offer much more than adding to our vitamin and nutrient consumption. They're colorful and they come in a broad spectrum of tastes and textures. If they're prepared in interesting ways, they can be standouts, enhancing a plain roast beef, chicken breast, or vegetarian main course and making an entire dinner more exciting and tempting.

BRAISED BEANS, TOMATOES, AND PEPPERS

(P)

One of the old collectible cookbooks in my collection, a book from the 1920s, advises the reader to cook string (green) beans for 1½ hours! No wonder whole generations of people grew up hating vegetables. It took until the late twentieth century for us to learn to keep vegetables crisp, "almost done." And yet, this particular string-bean dish is better when the beans have braised to softness and spent some time melding flavors with the onions and tomatoes.

1 pound (455 g) green string beans	3 medium tomatoes, chopped
1/4 cup (60 ml) olive oil	1/4 cup (15 g) chopped fresh parsley
1 medium onion, chopped	Salt, to taste
1/2 cup (75 g) chopped red bell pepper	1/2 teaspoon sugar
1 teaspoon chopped jalapeño pepper, optional	1/8 teaspoon cayenne pepper
2 cloves garlic, chopped	2 tablespoons (30 ml) lemon juice

Rinse the string beans, cut off and discard the ends, and cut the beans into 1½- to 2-inch (3.8- to 5-cm) pieces. Heat the olive oil in a sauté pan over medium heat. Add the onion, red pepper, jalapeño pepper, and green beans and cook for 3 minutes, stirring occasionally. Add the garlic and cook briefly. Cover the pan and cook for 3 to 4 minutes or until the beans are almost tender. Add the tomatoes, parsley, salt, sugar, and cayenne pepper and stir the ingredients. Cover and cook for another 3 to 4 minutes or until the vegetables are soft. Sprinkle with the lemon juice.

Yield: Makes 4 servings

SERVING SUGGESTIONS AND VARIATIONS: I have served this dish with poultry, meat, and fish. It would also be a good choice for a meatless or vegetarian meal paired with mashed potatoes, roasted cauliflower, cooked egg noodles, polenta, mushroom ragout, and so on—or even as an accompaniment to scrambled eggs.

CARROTS WITH HONEY, SCALLIONS, AND HOT PEPPER

(P)

When my children were babies, one of the first solid foods I remember introducing them to was carrots. It was a cinch: Peel a carrot, boil it up, mash it, and voilà! you're all set for a few wholesome, homemade infant meals. Most babies love carrots, which are among the sweeter vegetables. Grownups like them for the same reason. Fresh ginger and orange peel make this dish a refreshing riff on simple, boiled carrots. I like to serve these with plain roasted chicken so it can stand out as a side dish.

1 pound (455 g) carrots
2 tablespoons (40 g) honey
1½ tablespoons (21 g) coconut oil
2 scallions, finely chopped
1 teaspoon grated lime peel
1 teaspoon finely chopped chile pepper
Salt, to taste

Preheat the oven to 450°F (230°C, or gas mark 8). Line a cookie sheet with parchment paper. Peel the carrots and cut them into 1/2-inch (1.3-cm) slices. Place them on the parchment paper. Heat the honey and coconut oil together over low heat until the coconut oil has melted. Pour over the carrots. Sprinkle with the scallions, lime peel, and chile pepper. Sprinkle with salt. Toss the carrots to coat them completely. Roast for about 15 minutes, turning the carrots once or twice, until they are hot, tender, and crispy.

Yield: Makes 4 servings

DID YOU KNOW? Scientists and nutritionists used to warn us against coconut oil as an artery-clogging, heart-attack-in-the-making fat to avoid. New evidence shows that unrefined coconut oil is actually heart-healthy and may have other health benefits as well.

BRUSSELS SPROUTS WITH CHORIZO AND ONION

Chorizo is a hearty match for these robust cabbage cousins. This is a nice side dish for grilled steak or roast beef.

18 to 20 medium Brussels sprouts
2 tablespoons (30 ml) olive oil
1 chorizo sausage, chopped
1 Spanish or Vidalia onion, chopped
Salt and freshly ground black
pepper, to taste

Trim the bottoms of the Brussels sprouts and discard any discolored leaves. Cut the sprouts in half and soak them in cold water for about 10 minutes; drain and set aside.

Heat the olive oil in a sauté pan over medium heat. Add the chorizo and cook, stirring occasionally, for 2 to 3 minutes or until crispy. Remove the pieces with a slotted spoon and set aside.

Add the onion and Brussels sprouts to the pan and cook, stirring occasionally, for 4 to 5 minutes. Cover the pan and cook for another minute or until the Brussels sprouts are tender. Return the chorizo to the pan. Mix to reheat. Season with the salt and pepper.

Yield: Makes 4 servings

SERVING SUGGESTIONS AND VARIATIONS: You can use either spicy or mild chorizo, but if you prefer, make this dish with about 4 slices of Facon or beef bacon: Fry the bacon first and decrease the olive oil to 1 tablespoon (15 ml); use the bacon fat in place of the remaining tablespoon (15 ml) olive oil.

ROASTED HARISSA-GLAZED POTATOES (P)

Small new or baby Red Bliss potatoes are almost infallible. Whether you boil them, fry them, roast them, cook them plain, or cook them with a smear of olive oil and a sprinkle of salt, the result approaches perfection. They go with just about any meat main course and make a good side dish for an easy dinner of scrambled or sunny-side up eggs. It doesn't take much to dress them up either. In this recipe, I've included chopped scallion, parsley, and a coating of harissa to give them just a bit of heat.

1½ pounds (680 g) new potatoes
3 tablespoons (45 ml) olive oil
1 tablespoon (15 ml) lemon juice
2 teaspoons fresh thyme leaves
Salt, to taste
2 scallions, chopped
1 tablespoon (15 g) harissa

Preheat the oven to 375°F (190°C, or gas mark 5). Line a baking sheet with foil or parchment paper. Cut the potatoes into quarters and place them on the baking sheet. Mix the olive oil, lemon juice, and thyme and pour the dressing over the potatoes. Toss to coat the potatoes completely. Sprinkle with salt. Roast for 30 minutes or until tender and crispy brown, turning the potatoes once or twice during roasting. Add the scallions and harissa, toss the potatoes to spread the ingredients evenly, and roast for another 10 minutes.

Yield: Makes 4 servings

ROASTED TOMATOES WITH GOAT CHEESE AND THYME

(D)

This dish is best at the height of tomato season, near summer's end. But the goat cheese and thyme pack in so much flavor that even winter supermarket tomatoes can't spoil it.

4 large beefsteak tomatoes

3 tablespoons (45 ml) olive oil, divided

3/4 cup (90 g) plain bread crumbs

3/4 cup (112 g) crumbled goat cheese

2 teaspoons fresh thyme leaves

2 cloves garlic, finely chopped

Salt and freshly ground black pepper, to taste

Preheat the oven to 400°F (200°C, or gas mark 6). Line a cookie sheet with parchment paper. Cut the tomatoes in half. Remove the flesh and seeds, chop, and spoon them into a bowl. Discard any excess liquid inside the hollowed tomatoes. Brush the outside surfaces of the tomatoes with about 1/2 tablespoon (7.5 ml) of the olive oil.

Add the bread crumbs, cheese, thyme, and garlic to the bowl with the tomato flesh and seeds. Spoon equal amounts of this mixture inside the tomatoes. Drizzle the tops with the remaining olive oil and sprinkle with salt and pepper. Place the filled tomatoes on the cookie sheet. Bake for 20 minutes or until the tomatoes are tender and the stuffing is golden brown.

Yield: Makes 4 servings

SERVING SUGGESTIONS AND VARIATIONS: You can prepare these ahead of time. Just keep them refrigerated until you're ready to bake them. This is a good side dish with grilled fish, eggs, or other vegetarian dishes. You can use feta or blue cheese instead of goat cheese.

HOT-AND-SOUR NAPA CABBAGE

(P)

You'll have to think ahead to make this recipe! It's a kind of hot-and-spicy, sweet-and-sour "sauerkraut" and needs some time to soften and mellow.

1½ pounds (680 g) Napa cabbage
(or use green cabbage)

2 teaspoons salt

3 tablespoons (45 ml) vegetable oil

1 small serrano pepper, deseeded and finely chopped

1½ tablespoons (9 g) finely chopped fresh ginger

Freshly ground black pepper, to taste

¼ cup (60 ml) cider vinegar

1 tablespoon (15 ml) mirin

2½ tablespoons (32 g) sugar

> **TIP**
> To weigh down the cabbage, place a saucepan on top of the paper towels and put a couple of heavy cans inside the pan.

Cut the cabbage in half and remove the hard core. Shred the cabbage and place the pieces in a large bowl. Sprinkle with the salt and toss. Cover the bowl with paper towels and place a weight on top. Let rest for about 5 hours.

Rinse the shredded cabbage under cold water, drain, squeeze the shreds dry, and set aside. Heat the vegetable oil in a large sauté pan over medium-high heat. Add the serrano pepper, ginger, and a few gratings of pepper and stir for about 15 seconds. Add the cabbage and stir-fry for about 2 minutes. Add the vinegar, mirin, and sugar and stir-fry for another minute. Serve hot, cool, or at room temperature.

Yield: Makes 4 to 6 servings

DID YOU KNOW? Cabbage has a lot going for it. It's nourishing (loaded with vitamin C), cheap, easy to grow, and thrives in every climate. It is ubiquitous and so useful that people throughout most of the world eat it.

MAPLE AND ORANGE GLAZED PARSNIPS

Parsnips are underused and undervalued, and I have no idea why! I cook them often because they lend themselves to all sorts of cooking methods and seasonings. This recipe brings out the vegetable's natural sweet flavor.

1 pound (455 g) medium parsnips

1/2 cup (120 ml) water

1/2 cup (120 ml) orange juice

2 tablespoons (30 ml) maple syrup

2 tablespoons (28 g) Earth Balance Buttery Spread

Salt, to taste

2 tablespoons (6 g) chopped fresh chives

TIP

Choose medium-size parsnips because the large, thick ones can be woody and fibrous.

Peel the parsnips and cut them into strips about 1/4-inch (6-mm) thick and 3 inches (7.5-cm) long. Remove any fibrous, hard inner core. Place the water, orange juice, maple syrup, Buttery Spread, and salt in a large saucepan and bring to a boil over medium-high heat. Add the parsnips, cover the pan, and simmer for 5 to 8 minutes or until the parsnips are tender. Remove the parsnips with a slotted spoon and set aside.

Raise the heat and boil the pan liquid for 3 to 4 minutes or until syrupy. Return the parsnips to the pan and cook them until hot. Place the parsnips in a serving dish and sprinkle with chives.

Yield: Makes 4 servings

ROASTED CAULIFLOWER "STEAKS" Ⓟ

Cauliflower is milder than most of the other vegetables in the cabbage family. I've cooked it all sorts of ways: sometimes to tame it, sometimes to bring out a robust flavor. Roasting caramelizes the outside and gives the cauliflower a nutty flavor and satisfyingly crispy surface.

1 small head cauliflower

3 tablespoons (45 ml) olive oil

2 tablespoons (30 ml) lemon juice

1 teaspoon Dijon mustard

1/2 teaspoon sriracha

1 large clove garlic, finely chopped

2 teaspoons fresh thyme leaves

Salt, to taste

Preheat the oven to 400°F (200°C, or gas mark 6). Line a cookie sheet with parchment paper. Remove the green leaves at the bottom of the cauliflower and trim most of the fibrous stem attached to the head. Slice the head into "steaks," about 3/8-inch (1-cm) thick. Rinse and dry the slices on paper towels.

Combine the olive oil, lemon juice, mustard, sriracha, garlic, and thyme in a bowl. Brush this on both sides of the cauliflower slices. Place the slices on the parchment. Sprinkle with salt. Roast for 15 minutes. Turn the slices over and roast for another 10 to 15 minutes or until tender and crispy.

Yield: Makes 4 servings

SERVING SUGGESTIONS AND VARIATIONS: Sriracha provides some heat, but if you prefer less spice, don't add it; the dish is perfectly tasty without it.

STIR-FRIED BROCCOLI AND SHIITAKE MUSHROOMS

(P)

I always have broccoli in the house. It doesn't take much to dress it up into something special.

2 stalks broccoli

12 medium, fresh shiitake mushrooms

2 tablespoons (30 ml) olive oil

1/4 cup (40 g) chopped shallots

1/2 teaspoon crushed red pepper flakes

1/2 cup (120 ml) vegetable stock

Salt and freshly ground pepper, to taste

Remove about 1-inch (2.5-cm) from the bottom of the broccoli stems. Peel the stems and cut them and the florets into bite-size pieces. Cook the broccoli in lightly salted simmering water for about 2 minutes or until barely tender. Drain under cold water and set aside.

Remove and discard the mushroom stems; rinse the caps and chop them coarsely. Heat the olive oil in a sauté pan over medium heat. Add the shallots and shiitake mushrooms and cook, stirring occasionally, for 3 to 4 minutes. Add the red pepper flakes and broccoli and pour in the stock. Bring to a boil and cook, stirring occasionally, until most of the liquid evaporates. Sprinkle with salt and pepper.

Yield: Makes 4 servings

TIP

Don't discard broccoli stems! They have lots of flavor and aren't stringy and fibrous if you peel them. Here's how: Remove the florets with a small sharp knife. Cut about an inch (2.5 cm) off the bottom of the stem. Starting with that cut, peel back the thick outer skin toward the top (where the florets were).

ROASTED SWEET POTATOES AND APPLES

Ⓟ

Sweet potatoes are naturally sweet, so they don't need piles of brown sugar or other sweeteners to make them taste good. This dish has just a bit of maple syrup and gets extra sweetness and flavor from roasted apples and juice. It's one of my go-to dishes (a Thanksgiving must!) because I can make it ahead by a day or so.

3 pounds (1.4 kg) sweet potatoes

2 large apples, preferably baking apples

2 tablespoons (28 g) Earth Balance Buttery Spread or margarine

2 tablespoons (28 g) coconut oil

2 tablespoons (30 ml) maple syrup

1/2 teaspoon ground ginger

1/2 teaspoon ground cinnamon

Approximately 1/2 cup (120 ml) orange or tangerine juice

Salt, to taste

Preheat the oven to 400°F (200°C, or gas mark 6). Roast the sweet potatoes for 55 to 60 minutes or until tender. Part way through the roasting period, peel the apples, cut them into quarters, remove the core and seeds, and wrap the quarters in aluminum foil. Roast the apples in the same oven as the sweet potatoes for about 30 minutes or until tender.

When cool enough to handle, cut the sweet potatoes in half and scoop out the flesh into a bowl. Add the apples and any accumulated juices. Mash the sweet potatoes and apples together. Add the Buttery Spread, coconut oil, maple syrup, ginger, and cinnamon. Mash and mix thoroughly to blend the ingredients. Add some of the orange juice, using enough to mix the ingredients to the desired consistency. Season with salt. Place in a casserole dish to reheat (at 400°F [200°C, or gas mark 6]).

Yield: Makes 8 servings

DID YOU KNOW? Sweet potatoes are sometimes marketed as yams. No matter what the store sign states, these are different varieties of sweet potatoes. Yams are not grown commercially in the United States.

chapter

9

BREAKFAST, BRUNCH, AND SANDWICHES

People say they like breakfast but how many of us actually eat one during the week? We tend to skip this meal or grab a muffin or doughnut and call it breakfast. Most of us are more likely to satisfy our morning food needs over the weekend when there's more time to cook and enjoy a relaxed meal. This chapter offers recipes for foods that are welcome for breakfast, or brunch if it's late in the day, and all are suitable for company. Sandwiches also? Yes—they are suitable for any meal at all: breakfast, brunch, lunch, and even dinner!

BANANA BREAD WITH KEFIR AND ORANGE MARMALADE

(D)

Besides being a healthy, refreshing beverage, kefir is perfect for smoothies (add a few strawberries or a banana or mango) or in baked goods such as this banana bread.

2 cups (250 g) all-purpose flour

1 teaspoon baking soda

/2 teaspoon baking powder

/2 teaspoon salt

1 teaspoon ground cinnamon

/4 teaspoon freshly grated nutmeg

1 teaspoon grated fresh orange peel

3/4 cup (150 g) sugar

1/3 cup (75 g) coconut oil, melted

3 tablespoons (45 ml) vegetable oil

2 large eggs

3 medium, very ripe bananas, mashed

3 tablespoons (60 g) orange marmalade

1/4 cup (60 ml) kefir

1 teaspoon vanilla extract

Preheat the oven to 350°F (180°C, or gas mark 4). Grease a 9 x 5 x 3-inch (23 x 13 x 7.5-cm) loaf pan. Mix the flour, baking soda, baking powder, salt, cinnamon, nutmeg, and orange peel in a bowl and set aside. Beat the sugar and coconut and vegetable oils with a handheld or electric mixer set at medium speed for 2 to 3 minutes or until the mixture is well blended. Add the eggs one at a time, beating after each addition. Add the bananas and orange marmalade and beat the mixture to blend the ingredients thoroughly. Add the flour mixture, stirring only enough to blend in the dry ingredients. Stir in the kefir and vanilla extract. Spoon the batter into the prepared pan and bake for 50 to 60 minutes or until a cake tester inserted into the center comes out clean. Cool the bread in the pan for 15 minutes, then invert onto a cake rack to cool completely.

Yield: Makes 1 loaf

DID YOU KNOW? Kefir is an ancient beverage, discovered thousands of years ago by nomadic shepherds. They carried milk in leather bags and after a long day the liquid would ferment, turn sour, and develop tiny bubbles. Turns out it was a refreshing, revitalizing treat after a long day. Today we know kefir is a healthy probiotic and still quite tasty!

GRILLED CHEESE, EGG, AND AVOCADO PANINI WITH SRIRACHA MAYO

(D)

I can't imagine a grilled cheese sandwich that I wouldn't like. This one is a good pick for brunch because it's so attractive and also substantial. The rye bread adds extra flavor, especially the kind with seeds.

5 teaspoons (23 g) butter, divided

2 large eggs

2 tablespoons (28 g) mayonnaise

1/2 teaspoon sriracha

4 slices rye bread

3 to 4 ounces (85 to 115 g) Monterey Jack cheese, sliced

4 to 6 tomato slices

1/2 ripe Haas avocado, peeled and sliced

1 tablespoon (3 g) chopped fresh chives

> ## TIP
> You don't need a special panini pan. All you have to do is weight the sandwich down while it's cooking.

Heat 2 teaspoons butter in a sauté pan over medium heat. Crack the eggs and place them in the pan. Cook until the whites are set and barely crispy. Flip the eggs and cook for 30 to 45 seconds. Set aside. Mix the mayonnaise and sriracha together. Spread equal amounts of the mayonnaise on each of two slices of bread. Top with equal amounts of cheese, tomato, and avocado slices. Scatter the chives on top. Place one egg on top of each sandwich. Cover with second piece of bread. Heat 1½ teaspoons butter in the sauté pan over medium heat. When the butter has melted and looks foamy, place the sandwiches in the pan. Place another, heavier pan on top. Cook for about 2 minutes or until the bottoms are crispy-brown. Remove the heavier pan, lift the sandwiches with a spatula, and place them on a dish or cutting board. Add the remaining butter to the pan. When the butter has melted, add the sandwiches on the uncooked side and weight the sandwiches down with the heavier pan. Cook for another minute or so until second side is golden brown.

Yield: Makes 2 servings

SERVING SUGGESTIONS AND VARIATIONS: Although rye bread has a unique flavor that highlights the other ingredients in this sandwich, any bread will do. And any meltable cheese will be fine if you don't have Monterey Jack.

DOUBLE CORN FRITTERS WITH SCALLION AND CHILE PEPPER

(D)

I sometimes daydream about corn fritters, which I don't have very often because I think of them as an indulgence, like fried chicken and macaroni and cheese. These are among the foods that I think of as "happy" because when my mother made them, they always made me feel happy. In addition to their emotional appeal, corn fritters are pleasurable because they're soft and tender but have that terrific crispy edge.

2 tablespoons (28 g) butter or margarine	2 chopped scallions
1 cup (125 g) all-purpose flour	1 teaspoon finely chopped chile pepper
1/4 cup (36 g) cornmeal	1 cup (164 g) corn kernels
2 teaspoons baking powder	1 cup (235 ml) milk or refrigerated coconut milk
1 teaspoon salt	1 large egg
3/4 teaspoon sugar	Vegetable oil, for sautéing

Melt the butter and set it aside to cool. In a bowl, mix the flour, cornmeal, baking powder, salt, and sugar. Stir in the scallions and chile pepper and mix to distribute the ingredients evenly. Stir in the corn. In another bowl mix the milk, egg, and cooled melted butter. Pour the liquid into the flour mixture and stir to blend ingredients. Heat about 1/4-inch (6-mm) vegetable oil in a large sauté pan over medium high heat. Drop the batter by the quarter-cupful into the pan. Cook for about 2 minutes per side or until golden. Drain on paper towels.

Yield: Makes 16 to 20 fritters

SERVING SUGGESTIONS AND VARIATIONS: You can make all sorts of changes to the recipe: Add a few crumbles of cheese (feta, cottage, Parmesan) or make it parve by substituting Earth Balance Buttery Spread for the butter and unsweetened refrigerator-case coconut milk for the dairy milk. I like the parve version with fried chicken. The dairy version is a better brunch dish accompanied by sunny-side eggs because the fritter soaks up some of the rich, runny yolk.

FRITTATA WITH ONIONS, POTATOES, GREENS, AND CHEESE

(D)

Here is one of life's guarantees: Any time you put eggs, onions, and potatoes together, something delicious will come of it. For this frittata I've also included some colorful—and healthy—greens, plus cheese.

2 medium Yukon gold potatoes

8 large eggs

3 tablespoons (45 ml) milk, cream, or dairy sour cream

2 tablespoons (7.5 g) chopped fresh parsley

Salt and freshly ground black pepper, to taste

2 tablespoons (30 ml) vegetable oil

2 1/2 tablespoons (28 g) butter, divided

1 large onion, chopped

1 cup (60 g) packed, chopped fresh greens

3/4 cup (112 g) grated cheese (Swiss, Cheddar, mozzarella, or Monterey Jack)

Preheat the oven to 375°F (190°C, or gas mark 5). Peel the potatoes, cut them into small dice, and cook in lightly salted boiling water for 2 to 3 minutes or until slightly softened. Drain and set aside. Beat the eggs, milk, and parsley in a bowl, sprinkle with salt and pepper, and set aside. Heat the vegetable oil and 1/2 tablespoon of the butter in a sauté pan over medium heat. When the butter has melted and looks foamy, add the onion and cook for 2 minutes or until it has softened. Add the potatoes and cook for about 5 to 6 minutes or until the pieces are lightly crispy, stirring occasionally. Add the greens and cook for another minute, stirring occasionally. Dish out and set aside. Heat the remaining 2 tablespoons (28 g) butter in the pan. When it has melted and looks foamy, return the vegetables to the pan and pour in the egg mixture. Scatter the cheese on top. Stir to distribute the ingredients evenly. Turn the heat to low. Cook undisturbed for 3 to 4 minutes, or until the bottom has set. Place the pan in the oven and bake for 8 to 10 minutes, until the eggs are set.

Yield: Makes 4 servings

SERVING SUGGESTIONS AND VARIATIONS: You can use any kind of greens such as chard, kale, spinach, or beet greens. You can also add some sliced mushrooms (cook them with the onions).

MERGUEZ SHAKSHUKA

(M)

I love that the runny egg yolks ooze into the soft stew, enriching the meat and vegetables and mellowing the spiciness. This is usually a vegetarian dish, but the crispy bits of lamb sausage and Middle East seasonings add a new dimension to the classic version.

3 tablespoons (45 ml) olive oil

1 pound (455 g) Merguez sausage, cut into small pieces

1 medium onion, chopped

1 red bell pepper, deseeded and chopped

1 Cubanelle or other mild pepper, deseeded and chopped

1 large garlic clove, chopped

4 large tomatoes, coarsely chopped

1 teaspoon ras el hanout

1 teaspoon Aleppo pepper or 1/2 teaspoon crushed red pepper

8 large eggs

TIP

Watch out when you work with chile peppers! Use thin, disposable gloves or wash your hands several times before you attempt to insert contact lenses or touch any part of your face, mouth, or eyes.

Heat the olive oil in a large sauté pan over medium heat. Add the sausage and cook for 4 to 5 minutes to crisp the meat slightly. Add the onion and peppers and cook for 4 to 5 minutes or until softened. Add the garlic and cook briefly. Add the tomatoes, ras el hanout, and Aleppo pepper. Stir, cover the pan, turn the heat to low, and cook for 8 to 10 minutes, or until the vegetables are very soft, stirring occasionally. Crack the eggs into a small bowl one at a time and then transfer each one next to the other over the vegetables. Cover the pan and cook for 4 to 5 minutes or until the eggs are set but yolks are still slightly runny. Serve each person 2 eggs and some of the sausage and vegetables.

Yield: Makes 4 servings

SERVING SUGGESTIONS AND VARIATIONS: Aleppo pepper is mildly hot and vaguely smoky. If you can't find it, use crushed red pepper, harissa, sriracha, or cayenne pepper, to taste.

OATMEAL PANCAKES WITH ROASTED ORANGES

(D)

Ed and I have this running argument about which is better: thick, American-style flapjack pancakes or thin, French-style crepes. I like the thick. He likes the thin. But we both agree on this recipe: When you add cooked cereal, the pancakes are hearty rather than delicate. This recipe is a good way to use up any leftover oatmeal from yesterday's breakfast. The roasted oranges give it some glamour (plus vitamin C).

3 oranges, preferably juice (Valencia type) oranges

4 tablespoons (56 g) butter, plus more to cook the pancakes

Ground cinnamon, to taste

1 cup (225 g) cooked oatmeal, any kind

2 large eggs

1 cup (235 ml) milk

2 tablespoons (40 g) honey

1½ teaspoons vanilla extract

1½ cups (190 g) all-purpose flour

1½ teaspoons baking powder

½ teaspoon salt

Preheat the oven to 375°F (190°C, or gas mark 5). Cut the oranges into 6 segments each. Remove any obvious seeds. Melt the butter. Brush the fleshy part of the oranges with 1 tablespoon (15 ml) of the melted butter (let the remaining butter cool). Place the segments on a cookie sheet. Sprinkle lightly with cinnamon. Roast the oranges for 18 to 20 minutes or until lightly browned. Set aside. Place the oatmeal in a bowl. Add the eggs, milk, honey, vanilla extract, and remaining melted butter and mix to blend the ingredients thoroughly. Add the flour, baking powder, and salt and mix them in to make a relatively smooth batter. Melt a small amount of butter in a sauté pan over medium heat. When the butter has melted and looks foamy, drop about ¼ cup (60 ml) of the batter onto the pan for each pancake, leaving space between each one. Cook the pancakes for 1 to 2 minutes or until golden brown on the bottom. Turn the pancakes over and cook on the second side for 1 to 2 minutes or until browned. Serve plain or with syrup and a few segments of roasted orange.

Yield: Makes about 6 servings (about 18 small pancakes)

SERVING SUGGESTIONS AND VARIATIONS: You can change this to parve by substituting coconut milk and margarine for the milk and butter.

SALMON, EGG, AND SWISS CHARD MELTS WITH TARRAGON BUTTER

(D)

Artisanal breads have been the darlings of the food world in the last few years, but good, old-fashioned rye bread, with its crunchy crust and spicy caraway seeds, has a lot to offer, too, especially here, combined with rich salmon and cheese.

4 large slices rye bread

2 tablespoons (28 g) butter, slightly softened

2 teaspoons chopped fresh tarragon

1/2 cup (90 g) packed chopped Swiss chard leaves (about 2 large leaves)

8 slices tomato

2 hard cooked eggs, sliced

4 ounces (115 g) cooked salmon

1/2 cup (55 g) shredded Swiss cheese

2 tablespoons (10 g) grated Parmesan cheese

TIP

You can prepare these up to a day ahead (keep them refrigerated) and heat them for serving just before you need them.

Preheat the oven to 400°F (200°C, or gas mark 6). Lightly toast the bread and set it aside. Mix the butter and tarragon and spread equal amounts on each of the bread slices. Place the slices on a cookie sheet. Layer equal amounts of chard, tomato, and egg on top. Cut the salmon into 4 equal portions and place on top of the tomato. Scatter the Swiss cheese over the fish. Sprinkle with Parmesan cheese. Bake for 3 to 4 minutes or until the cheese is hot and bubbly.

Yield: Makes 4 melts, or 2 to 4 servings

SERVING SUGGESTIONS AND VARIATIONS: Freshly cooked or leftover salmon is best, but sometimes I use canned salmon for this recipe. Any green will do if you don't have chard: Try spinach, kale, or beet greens.

PUMPKIN MUFFINS

These are probably my favorite of favorite muffins. They are amazingly tender and yet have that little bit of contrasting crunch on top from the pumpkin seeds. Don't wait for autumn to make these. I don't! There are always some in my freezer so I can have a quick breakfast or coffee snack.

1 cup (245 g) pumpkin purée

1/2 cup (75 g) brown sugar

1/3 cup (67 g) white sugar

1/2 cup (120 ml) vegetable oil

1/3 cup (80 ml) coconut milk

2 large eggs

13/4 cups (167 g) all-purpose flour

1 teaspoon baking soda

3/4 teaspoon salt

1/2 teaspoon ground cinnamon

1/2 teaspoon grated fresh nutmeg

1/4 teaspoon ground ginger

3 tablespoons (45 g) slightly crushed toasted pumpkin seeds

TIP

Use homemade mashed pumpkin or canned pumpkin, not pumpkin pie mix, which has spices already mixed in.

Preheat the oven to 350°F (180°C, or gas mark 4). Lightly grease 9 to 10 muffin tin cups. Combine the pumpkin purée, sugars, vegetable oil, and coconut milk in a large bowl and whisk the ingredients for 1 to 2 minutes or until thoroughly blended. Whisk in the eggs. Combine the flour, baking soda, salt, cinnamon, nutmeg, and ginger and add them to the pumpkin mixture. Whisk the ingredients for 1 to 2 minutes or until thoroughly blended. Spoon equal amounts of the batter into the prepared muffin tin cups. Sprinkle equal amounts of the pumpkin seeds on top of each muffin. Bake for 25 to 30 minutes or until a cake tester inserted into the center of the muffins comes out clean.

Yield: Makes 9 to 10 muffins

CHALLAH

(P)

I've written about my grandma's famous challah many times, and everyone I know suggested I include it in this book, so here it is. Grandma's recipe was typical of its time and included such items as "8 hands of flour, 1/2 hand sugar, small glass oil." No instructions. It took me a while to figure it out, but it was worth it. This is my most requested recipe, the most requested food item I am asked to bring to anything. My grandma won an award for it back in the day. Try it and you'll know why.

2 packages active dry yeast

1/2 cup (120 ml) warm water (105°F to 110°F, or 41°C to 43°C)

1/2 cup (100 g) sugar, divided

8 to 8 1/2 cups (1 to 1.1 kg) all-purpose flour, divided

1 tablespoon (18 g) salt

5 large eggs, divided

3 tablespoons (45 ml) vegetable oil

1 1/2 cups (355 ml) lukewarm water (about 100°F, or 38°C)

1 teaspoon water

Poppy seeds or sesame seeds, optional

Preheat the oven to 350°F (180°C, or gas mark 4). In a small bowl, mix the yeast, the 1/2 cup (120 ml) warm water, 1/2 teaspoon of the sugar, and a pinch of flour. Stir, set aside, and let rest for 5 minutes or until the mixture becomes bubbly.

In a bowl of an electric mixer, combine 7 1/2 cups (938 g) flour with the remaining sugar and the salt. In a small bowl, mix 4 of the eggs, the vegetable oil, and the lukewarm water. Add to the flour mixture. Add the yeast mixture and blend thoroughly. Using the kneading hook, knead for 4 to 5 minutes or until the dough is smooth and elastic, adding more flour as necessary to make sure the dough is not sticky. *Note:* You can make this dough in a food processor (halve the recipe).

Cover the bowl of dough and put it in a warm place to rise for about 1 1/2 hours or until doubled in bulk. Punch down the dough, cover the bowl, and let rise again for about 45 minutes or until doubled. Remove the dough to a floured surface.

Cut the dough into 6 pieces. Make long strands out of the pieces. Braid the strands (see sidebar). Place the braided dough on a lightly greased cookie sheet. Beat the last egg with the teaspoon of water. Brush this over the surface of the bread. Sprinkle with seeds, if desired. Let rise again for 30 minutes.

Bake for 35 to 40 minutes (the bread should be firm and golden brown and make a hollow sound when you knock on the surface; with an instant read thermometer the temperature should measure 190°F [88°C]).

Yield: Makes 1 large challah, or 16 servings

SERVING SUGGESTIONS AND VARIATIONS: This makes a very large challah, which we always need because no one can eat just one piece. But you can halve the recipe (or make two smaller loaves). Shorten the baking time (about 30 to 35 minutes).

DID YOU KNOW? You probably do know that leftover challah makes the best French toast.

Braiding a Six-Strand Challah:

Place the six strands in front of you and gather them at the top end. Press down and seal the six strands at the top so it looks like a lump of dough with six strands coming down. Looking at the strands, proceed as follows:

1. Place the far-right strand all the way over to the left.
2. Place the former far-left strand all the way over to the right.
3. Place the now far-left strand into the middle.
4. Place the second strand from the right to the far left.
5. Place the now far right into the middle.
6. Place the second from left to far right.
7. Place the now far left into the middle.

Repeat steps 4 through 7 until the strands are used up. Press the strands to seal the bottom of the loaf.

SALMON, CHEESE, AND MANGO WAFFLE PANINI

Wait until you see the surprised faces when you serve waffle paninis.
These sandwiches are lots of fun, especially for kids.

5½ tablespoons (77 g) butter, divided

1 tablespoon (11 g) Dijon mustard

8 frozen round regular waffles, at room temperature

8 to 12 slices fresh mango

1 small jalapeño pepper, deseeded
and chopped, optional

6 ounces (170 g) leftover cooked salmon

4 to 6 ounces (115 to 170 g) Cheddar cheese, sliced

TIP

Belgian waffles are
too thick for this
recipe. Stick with
regular waffles.

Combine 4 tablespoons (56 g) butter and the Dijon mustard and blend thoroughly. Spread equal amounts of the mixture on one side of the waffles. Top 4 of the buttered waffles with 2 to 3 slices of mango and the chopped jalapeño pepper, if used, then equal amounts of fish and Cheddar cheese. Cover with the remaining waffles, buttered side down. Heat half the remaining butter in a large sauté pan over medium heat. When the butter has melted and looks foamy, place the waffle sandwiches in the pan. Place another, heavier pan on top. Cook for about 2 minutes. Remove the heavier pan, lift the sandwiches with a spatula, and place them on a dish or cutting board. Add the remaining butter to the pan. When the butter has melted, add the sandwiches on the uncooked side and weigh the sandwiches down with the heavier pan. Cook for another 2 minutes or until the second side is golden brown.

Yield: Makes 4 servings

SERVING SUGGESTIONS AND VARIATIONS: Canned salmon is fine here, and if you don't have mango or don't like it, use fresh peaches or nectarines instead.

SPICY SCRAMBLED EGGS

(D)

This is an easy, colorful way to dress up plain old scrambled eggs. They're especially good served with warm flat breads such as naan or pita.

8 large eggs

1/2 cup (120 ml) milk

2 tablespoons (28 g) butter

1 tablespoon (15 ml) vegetable oil

4 scallions, chopped

16 grape tomatoes, cut into small pieces

2 tablespoons (10 g) chopped fresh cilantro

1 tablespoon (9 g) finely chopped fresh chile pepper

1 1/2 teaspoons chopped fresh ginger

1 large clove garlic, chopped

1/2 teaspoon ground cumin

1/4 teaspoon turmeric

Salt, to taste

Beat the eggs and milk together in a bowl; set aside. Heat the butter and vegetable oil in a large sauté pan over medium heat. When the butter has melted and looks foamy, add the scallions and cook briefly. Add the tomatoes, cilantro, chile pepper, ginger, garlic, cumin, and turmeric and cook, stirring occasionally, for about 2 minutes. Pour in the eggs, turn the heat to low and let the eggs set partially, then mix to scramble the ingredients together and cook to desired consistency. Season with salt.

Yield: Makes 4 servings

SERVING SUGGESTIONS AND VARIATIONS: This dish is spicy so you might want to temper the heat by serving it with baked or roasted potatoes. On the other hand, if you want to pile on spicy stuff, try it with Roasted Harissa-Glazed Potatoes, page 123.

chapter

....

10

BUDGET MEALS

Pinching pennies, using up leftovers, and eating less meat or less expensive cuts are all well-known ways to tighten our belts when we don't have heaps of money to spend on food. It can sound austere, and yet being mindful of what we eat and doing what we can to sustain the earth and its produce is at the very heart of kashruth. But even beyond the virtue of making use of scraps, bones, neglected cuts of meat, cooked vegetables from yesterday's dinner, stale bread, and such, this is a way to use our best culinary creativity to make something out of very little.

BEEF BACON, TOMATO, AND MUSHROOM PASTA

Ⓜ

Bacon has such an intense, smoky flavor that just a small amount of it gives a huge boost of flavor and a big splash to a dish such as this one.

1 pound (455 g) penne or ziti pasta

8 to 12 ounces (225 to 280 g) beef bacon

3 tablespoons (45 ml) olive oil

1 medium onion, chopped

1 large clove garlic, chopped

12 ounces (340 g) mushrooms, coarsely chopped

2 pounds (900 g) plum tomatoes, chopped

1 cup (130 g) frozen peas

3 tablespoons (11 g) chopped fresh parsley

1 to 2 pinches crushed red pepper

Cook the pasta according to the directions on the package, drain, and set aside. While the pasta is cooking, cut the bacon into 1/2-inch (1.3-cm) pieces and cook them in a large sauté pan over medium heat for 4 to 5 minutes or until crispy. Remove the bacon to a dish and set aside. Add the olive oil to the fat in the pan. Add the onion, garlic, and mushrooms and cook for 3 to 4 minutes or until softened. Add the tomatoes and cook, stirring often, for 2 to 3 minutes. Add the peas, parsley, and red pepper. Toss to distribute the ingredients evenly. Return the bacon to the pan. Add the cooked pasta and toss the ingredients. Cook for 1 to 2 minutes or until heated through.

Yield: Makes 4 servings

CHICKEN LIVER PO' BOYS

(M)

Po' boys are what folks in New Orleans call their hero, grinder, or submarine sandwiches. These sandwiches are often stuffed with fried food, including fried chicken livers.

1/2 cup (115 g) mayonnaise

1 chipotle pepper in adobo sauce, chopped

1 pound (455 g) chicken livers

3/4 cup (94 g) all-purpose flour

2 large eggs

1 teaspoon hot sauce, such as Tabasco

1 cup (145 g) cornmeal

1/2 teaspoon ground cumin

Salt and freshly ground black pepper, to taste

Vegetable oil, for frying

4 club rolls, Portuguese rolls, or one large Italian style bread

Lettuce

Tomato slices

Mix the mayonnaise and chipotle in adobo and refrigerate. Trim the livers and cut them into their natural sections. Dry them on paper towels. Place the flour in a dish. Beat the eggs and hot sauce in a second dish. Mix the cornmeal, cumin, salt, and pepper in a third dish. Coat the livers with the flour, then the egg mixture, then the cornmeal mixture. Set the livers aside to air-dry for about 15 minutes. Heat about 1/4 inch (6 mm) vegetable oil in a deep sauté pan over medium heat. When the oil is hot, fry the livers a few at a time for about 3 minutes per side or until crispy and browned. Drain on paper towels. Slice the rolls. Slather the bottoms with equal amounts of the mayonnaise mixture. Layer on a piece of lettuce and some tomato slices. Place equal amounts of the fried livers on top. Cover with the other part of the roll. Cut the sandwich into four equal parts if you made it on a whole Italian bread.

> **TIP**
>
> When you fry food, use a large pan; otherwise, your food will absorb too much grease. If your pan isn't big enough, fry in batches.

Yield: Makes 4 sandwiches

SERVING SUGGESTIONS AND VARIATIONS: You can put all sorts of add-ons into this sandwich: roasted red peppers, avocado slices, crispy beef bacon, sunny-side eggs, pickles, grilled onions, arugula, and coleslaw.

JANSSON'S SALMON TEMPTATION (D)

It may only be a legend, but I once read that this dish, with its tender potatoes, savory fish, and ultra-rich cream sauce, got its name because the leader of an austere Swedish-American religious community thought it was so delicious he couldn't stop himself from eating it, thereby breaking his vows to avoid temptations of the flesh. He got caught red-handed by a disillusioned member of his flock. Others say the dish is named after an opera star, while still others say it got its name from a movie. No matter, this is a substantial, inexpensive, and tempting dish, especially on a cold winter night.

6 medium all-purpose potatoes

2 tablespoons (30 ml) vegetable oil

4 tablespoons (56 g) butter, divided

2 large onions, sliced

2 cups (280 g) crumbled leftover salmon or other fish

Ground white pepper, to taste

1 cup (235 ml) half-and-half cream

1 cup (235 ml) whole milk

3/4 cup (38 g) fresh bread crumbs

TIP

Look at the casserole after the first 30 minutes of baking; if the top seems to be browning too quickly, cover loosely with aluminum foil (remove the foil for the last 5 minutes).

Preheat the oven to 400°F (200°C, or gas mark 6). Lightly grease a casserole dish. Peel the potatoes and cut them into thin slices. Set aside in a bowl and cover with cold water. Heat the vegetable oil with 1 tablespoon (15 ml) butter in a sauté pan over medium heat. When the butter has melted and looks foamy, add the onion and cook for 4 to 5 minutes or until it has softened. Remove the pan from the heat and set aside. Drain the potatoes, dry them with paper towels, and place one-third in a layer on the bottom of the casserole. Top with half the onion and half the salmon. Sprinkle with pepper. Repeat this layer, ending with a final layer of potato slices on top. Pour in the half-and-half and milk. Melt the remaining butter. Mix the bread crumbs and melted butter together and scatter on top of the potatoes. Bake for 50 to 60 minutes or until the potatoes are tender and liquid is almost completely absorbed.

Yield: Makes 4 to 6 servings

BLACK BEAN CAKES WITH CARAMELIZED ONIONS, PEPPERS, AND CHEESE

(D)

Several people in my family are vegetarians, so I always try to come up with something substantial and tasty for them when they're over for dinner. This has become a favorite, with or without the cheese, depending on the meal.

2 cans (15 ounces, or 425 g, each) black beans, drained and rinsed

3 scallions, finely chopped

2 small carrots, grated

2 medium garlic cloves, finely chopped

2 tablespoons (2 g) chopped fresh cilantro

1 large egg

1/2 cup (55 g) plain bread crumbs

Salt, to taste

1/8 teaspoon cayenne pepper

1/4 cup (36 g) cornmeal

Vegetable oil, for frying

1 red bell pepper, deseeded and sliced

1 medium sweet onion, sliced

1/2 cup (75 g) crumbled feta or goat cheese

Preheat the oven to warm. Mash the beans with a fork or in a food processor and place in a bowl. Add the scallions, carrots, garlic, cilantro, and egg. Mix to distribute the ingredients thoroughly. Add the bread crumbs and season with salt and cayenne pepper. Mix the ingredients thoroughly and shape into 8 patties. Coat the patties on both sides with cornmeal. Heat a small amount of vegetable oil in a sauté pan over medium heat. Fry the patties for 3 to 4 minutes per side or until lightly browned. Place the patties on a cookie sheet and keep warm in the oven. Pour about 2 tablespoons (30 ml) vegetable oil into the pan and place over medium heat. Add the bell pepper and onion and sauté for 4 to 6 minutes or until softened and lightly browned. Place the bean cakes on plates and surround them with the peppers and onions. Crumble the cheese over the peppers and onions and serve.

Yield: Makes 4 servings

SERVING SUGGESTIONS AND VARIATIONS: Serve these like hamburgers on a bun, or with sunny-side eggs, or as part of a vegetarian meal. It's also a good choice for brunch: Make them ahead and refrigerate. When ready to serve, reheat in a 400°F (200°C, or gas mark 6) oven. To make it into a parve dish, leave out the cheese.

LEMON-OREGANO STUFFED BREAST OF VEAL

(M)

Breast of veal looks regal, but it is reasonably priced compared with other cuts. The meat is lean but rich tasting and the stuffing makes this a filling and substantial dish.

5 tablespoons (45 ml) olive oil, divided

1 small onion, chopped

1/4 cup (15 g) chopped parsley

1 1/2 cups (75 g) fresh bread crumbs

1 large egg

Salt and freshly ground black pepper, to taste

Breast of veal, 3 to 4 pounds (1.4 kg to 1.8 kg), with pocket

1 teaspoon dried oregano

4 carrots, cut into chunks

2 large Yukon gold potatoes, peeled and cut into chunks

1 onion, cut into chunks

Juice of 2 lemons (about 1/2 cup, or 120 ml)

Preheat the oven to 350°F (180°C, or gas mark 4). Heat 2 tablespoons (30 ml) olive oil in a sauté pan over medium heat. Add the onion and cook for 4 to 5 minutes or until lightly browned. Remove from the heat. Add the parsley and bread crumbs to the pan and mix to distribute the ingredients evenly. Mix in the egg, salt, and pepper. Stuff the mixture into the pocket in the veal. Place the meat in a roasting pan. Coat the surface of the meat with 1 tablespoon (15 ml) olive oil. Scatter the oregano on top and season with salt and pepper. Place the carrots, potatoes, and onion chunks around the meat. Pour the remaining 2 tablespoons (30 ml) oil over the vegetables and toss them around the pan to coat them with the olive oil. Roast the meat for 30 minutes. Pour the lemon juice over the meat and vegetables. Roast for another hour or until the meat is crispy and cooked through (a meat thermometer will register 160°F [71°C]). Baste once or twice with pan juices during cooking time. Remove the meat and let rest for 10 to 15 minutes before slicing. Lower the oven heat to warm. Keep the vegetables warm in the oven while the meat rests.

Yield: Makes 4 servings

SERVING SUGGESTIONS AND VARIATIONS: This recipe is a meal-in-one because I've included roasted vegetables. You can add others such as Brussels sprouts, broccoli, or cauliflower.

ROASTED LAMB PROVENÇAL

Ⓜ

I love to gnaw on the bones of this dish!

4 pounds (1.8 kg) bone-in lamb
shoulder stew chunks

2 tablespoons (30 ml) olive oil

2 leeks, cleaned and finely chopped

1 large sweet onion, chopped

3 sprigs fresh thyme

2/3 cup (160 ml) chicken stock

1/3 cup (80 ml) white wine

Salt and freshly ground black pepper, to taste

4 carrots, cut into 1/2-inch (1.3-cm) slices

2 large Yukon gold potatoes, peeled and cut
into small chunks

3 tablespoons (11 g) chopped fresh parsley

TIP

I prefer to use stew meat with bones rather than boneless pieces, first because the bones add more flavor and second because the boneless pieces are usually too small. They shrink too much as they cook and can be rubbery.

Preheat the oven to 250°F (120°C, or gas mark 1/2). Rinse and dry the lamb. Heat the olive oil in a heat-proof pan over medium heat. Add the meat and cook, turning occasionally, for about 6 to 8 minutes or until browned on all sides. Remove the meat to a dish and set aside. Add the leeks and onion to the pan and cook for 5 to 6 minutes or until they are tender and beginning to brown. Remove the pan from the heat. Return the meat to the pan. Place the thyme sprigs in the pan. Pour in the stock and wine. Season with salt and pepper. Cover the pan. Place in the oven for 3 hours. Add the carrots, potatoes, and parsley and cook for another hour or until the meat is very soft and the vegetables are tender. Look occasionally inside the pan during cooking time and add more liquid if necessary.

Yield: Makes 4 servings

BRAISED KALE, TOMATO, AND CHEESE FRITTATA

After years of research, nutritionists and the American Heart Association now say it's okay to eat eggs—in moderation—because they're low in calories and loaded with high-quality protein. And consider the value: For the money, there's no better source of nutrients than an egg.

For the Braised Kale:

1 bunch kale, about 12 to 14 ounces (340 to 395 g)

2 tablespoons (30 ml) olive oil

1 clove garlic, sliced

1⅓ cups (315 ml) vegetable stock

Salt and freshly ground black pepper, to taste

For the Frittata:

2 tablespoons (28 g) butter

1 medium onion, chopped

1 cup (180 g) chopped grape tomatoes

2 cups (260 g) packed, chopped, braised kale (directions follow)

9 to 10 large eggs, beaten

½ cup (75 g) grated Cheddar cheese

Salt and freshly ground black pepper, to taste

Make the Braised Kale: Wash the kale thoroughly, discarding any thick, heavy stems. Dry the leaves with paper towels or in a salad spinner. Chop or tear the leaves coarsely. Heat the olive oil in a sauté pan over medium heat. Add the garlic and cook for about 1 minute, or until lightly browned. Remove and discard the garlic. Add the kale, stock, salt, and pepper and cook, covered, stirring occasionally, for 5 to 6 minutes or until the kale has wilted. Remove the cover and cook for another minute or until the liquid in the pan has evaporated. Makes 4 to 6 servings.

Make the Frittata: Preheat the oven to 375°F (190°C, or gas mark 5). Heat the butter in a sauté pan over medium heat. When the butter has melted and looks foamy, add the onion and cook for 2 to 3 minutes, stirring occasionally. Add the tomatoes and cook for another minute. Stir in the kale and mix to distribute the ingredients evenly. Pour in the eggs and turn the heat to low. Scatter the cheddar cheese on top. Stir once or twice, then cook undisturbed for 5 to 6 minutes, or until the bottom has set. Place the pan in the oven and bake for 8 to 10 minutes or until the eggs are set. Season with salt and pepper.

Yield: Makes 4 servings

SAUSAGE JAMBALAYA

Jambalaya is basically Creole-style rice pilaf with lots of extras—usually seafood and sometimes chicken or sausage, or all three. When I want to make a down-to-earth version of this dish, I use chorizo, because it has so much flavor that no other meats are needed.

2 tablespoons (30 ml) olive oil

1 pound (455 g) kosher chorizo sausage, cut into slices, 1/4 inch (6 mm) thick

2 large onions, chopped

2 stalks celery, chopped

1 medium red bell pepper, deseeded and chopped

3 large cloves garlic cloves, chopped

3 large tomatoes, chopped

1 1/2 cups (293 g) uncooked white rice

2 tablespoons (7.5 g) chopped parsley

1 1/2 teaspoons fresh thyme leaves

1/4 to 1/2 teaspoon cayenne pepper

1/8 teaspoon ground cloves

Salt and freshly ground black pepper, to taste

2 tablespoons (32 g) tomato paste

2 3/4 cups (630 ml) chicken or vegetable stock or water, or a combination

1 cup (130 g) frozen peas, thawed

Heat the olive oil in a large sauté pan over medium heat. Add the sausage and cook for 3 to 4 minutes, until lightly crispy. Remove the sausage to a plate. Add the onions, celery, and bell pepper to the pan and cook, stirring occasionally, for 3 to 4 minutes or until the vegetables have softened. Add the garlic and tomatoes and cook for 2 minutes. Add the rice, parsley, thyme, cayenne, cloves, salt, and pepper. Mix in the tomato paste. Pour in the stock and stir to combine the ingredients. Return the sausage to the pan. Bring the liquid to a boil. Lower the heat, cover the pan, and cook for about 30 minutes or until the rice is tender. Mix in the peas, cover the pan, let rest for 5 minutes and serve.

Yield: Makes 6 servings

SMOKED SALMON ENDS FRITTATA WITH VEGETABLE YOGURT DIP

Ⓓ

I never use expensive, hand-cut salmon for a dish such as this, where the fish is chopped into pieces. Fortunately, many stores sell the much cheaper salmon ends and scraps.

For the Smoked Salmon Ends Frittata:

8 large eggs

1/4 cup (60 ml) milk

Salt and freshly ground black pepper, to taste

2 tablespoons (28 g) butter, divided

1/3 cup (54 g) chopped red onion

8 to 10 chopped grape tomatoes

4 ounces (115 g) smoked salmon scraps

For the Vegetable Yogurt Dip:

1 cup (230 g) Greek style plain yogurt

2 chopped scallions or 1/4 cup (40 g) chopped red onion

2 to 3 radishes, finely chopped

2 tablespoons (15 g) finely chopped carrot

1 to 2 teaspoons lemon juice

Make the Smoked Salmon Ends Frittata: Preheat the oven to 375°F (190°C, or gas mark 5). Beat the eggs and milk in a bowl, sprinkle with salt and pepper, and set aside. Heat 1 tablespoon (14 g) butter in a sauté pan over medium heat. When the butter has melted and looks foamy, add the red onion and tomatoes and cook for 2 minutes or until softened. Add the remaining tablespoon (14 g) butter to the pan. When it has melted and looks foamy, pour in the eggs. Scatter the salmon on top. Stir to distribute the ingredients evenly. Turn the heat to low. Cook undisturbed for 3 to 4 minutes, or until the bottom has set. Place the pan in the oven and bake for 8 to 10 minutes, until the eggs are set.

Make the Vegetable Yogurt Dip: Place the yogurt, scallions, radishes, carrot, and lemon juice in a bowl and mix thoroughly. Spoon some of the dip on top of each serving of the frittata. Makes about 1 1/4 cups (330 g).

Yield: Makes 4 servings

BREAD AND TOMATO GRATIN

This recipe is proof of the culinary miracles you can conjure with simple, inexpensive ingredients such as bread, tomatoes, and cheese.

2 tablespoons (30 ml) olive oil

1 medium onion, chopped

2 cloves garlic, chopped

1 can (28 ounces, or 794 g, each) Italian style tomatoes, including liquid

2 tablespoons (5 g) chopped fresh basil

Salt and freshly ground black pepper, to taste

3 cups (105 g) stale Italian or French bread cubes (about 3/4-inch, or 1.9-cm, square)

1½ cups (175 g) shredded mozzarella cheese

1/2 cup (50 g) freshly grated Parmesan

Preheat the oven to 350°F (180°C, or gas mark 4). Lightly oil a 9-inch (23-cm) square baking dish. Heat the olive oil in a sauté pan over low-medium heat. Add the onion and cook for 6 to 8 minutes or until soft and beginning to brown. Add the garlic and cook briefly. Add the tomatoes, basil, salt, and pepper. Chop the tomatoes coarsely in the pan as they cook. Bring the liquid in the pan to a boil, reduce the heat, and simmer the ingredients for 10 minutes. Place half the bread cubes in the prepared baking dish, top with half the tomato mixture, half the mozzarella cheese, and half the Parmesan cheese. Repeat the layers. Bake for 25 to 30 minutes or until crispy and bubbling.

Yield: Makes 4 to 6 servings

SERVING SUGGESTIONS AND VARIATIONS: Although this casserole dish itself is filling, a first-course salad or soup would make it into a more substantial dinner.

THIS AND THAT SOUP

(M)

This is an amazingly flexible dish. I've made it dozens and dozens of times, adding a little of this or a little of that depending on what I have in the pantry or fridge. It's a terrific way to use leftovers and cheap, meaty bones. It cooks for hours and, as it simmers, it gives off that warm, comforting, welcoming smell that brings the family into the kitchen. It also freezes well.

5 dried shiitake mushrooms

2 leeks

3 to 4 pounds (1.4 to 1.8 kg) meaty bones

12 cups (3 L) water

1/2 cup (90 g) wheat berries, freekeh, or farro

1/2 cup (125 g) dried white beans

1/2 cup (102 g) split peas

1/2 cup (96 g) lentils

4 medium carrots, sliced

2 stalks celery, sliced

2 parsnips, sliced

8 sprigs fresh dill

6 sprigs fresh parsley

2 to 3 sprigs fresh thyme

Salt and freshly ground black pepper, to taste

Soak the mushrooms in hot water for 20 to 25 minutes or until softened, rinse them to remove any dirt, discard the stems, and chop the caps. Set aside. Remove and discard the dark green leaves from the leeks. Cut off the root. Split the leeks lengthwise. Rinse them under cold running water, separating the leaves to rid them of dirt and debris. Dry the leeks with paper towels, then chop and set them aside. Place the bones in a soup pot and cover with water. Bring to a boil over high heat. Lower the heat to a simmer and for the next several minutes, discard the debris that comes to the surface. Add the mushrooms, leeks, and remaining ingredients. Bring to a simmer and cook, partially covered, for 3 to 4 hours. Remove the bones and cut off bits of meat; discard the bones. Add the meat back to the soup, heat through, and serve.

Yield: Makes 8 servings

SERVING SUGGESTIONS AND VARIATIONS: You can make this with any meaty bones: chicken, veal, or beef. You can even use a leftover roasted chicken or turkey carcass.

PASSOVER DISHES

When it comes to Seder, most of us will likely cook our treasured family dishes. Everyone expects Grandma's matzo ball soup or the heirloom recipe for brisket. And yet, as time passes, children marry, families grow, new friends join in, and with that, other traditions to think about. There's also a growing awareness of eating lighter, healthier food, even at holiday time, and the need to consider those family members and friends who are vegetarians or who have special food concerns. A world of new dishes can be worked in alongside a family's traditional must-haves.

MASHED POTATO, KALE, AND FETA CHEESE PANCAKES

(D)

I think I could eat a hundred of these! They're soft and creamy inside, with that vaguely mineral-y mashed potato taste, but there's that crispy, golden brown surface, too! And tangy cheese and bitter kale! I like them plain for lunch or brunch, but for a bigger meal, I serve them with eggs or roasted vegetables.

2 cups (145 g) matzo farfel	2 cups (450 g) mashed potatoes
2 tablespoons (30 ml) olive oil	6 ounces (170 g) crumbled feta cheese
1 tablespoon (14 g) butter	1 large egg
1 medium onion, chopped	Salt and freshly ground pepper, to taste
2 cups (140 g) chopped fresh kale	Vegetable oil, for frying

Place the matzo farfel in a large bowl, cover with very hot water, and let soak for a few minutes until soft. Drain the farfel and squeeze out as much water as possible. Return the farfel to the bowl. While the farfel is soaking, heat the olive oil and butter in a sauté pan over medium heat. When the butter has melted and looks foamy, add the onion and cook for a minute. Add the kale, cover the pan, and continue to cook, stirring occasionally, for 5 to 6 minutes, or until the kale has wilted. Spoon the mixture into a strainer and squeeze out as much liquid as possible from the vegetables. Add to the matzo farfel and mix to distribute the ingredients evenly. Add the mashed potatoes, feta cheese, and egg and mix ingredients thoroughly. Season with salt and pepper. Heat about 1/2-inch (1.3-cm) vegetable oil in a large sauté pan over medium-high heat. Shape the potato mixture into patties and fry for 2 to 3 minutes per side, or until golden brown. Drain on paper towels.

Yield: Makes about 16 to 18 pancakes, or 6 to 8 servings

SERVING SUGGESTIONS AND VARIATIONS: Change this to a parve dish by substituting ground cooked meat or sausage for the cheese and frying the onion and kale in olive oil.

HAROSET WITH PISTACHIOS AND PEPPER

(P)

Haroset is one of the symbolic foods on the Seder plate, but in our family, we eat it as a relish with the meal. I've made dozens of versions over the years. This one is spicy, and my kids didn't like it at first. Now I double the recipe because it's everyone's favorite; we couldn't think of having a Seder without it.

1 cup (130 g) chopped dried apricots

1/2 cup (60 g) chopped dates

1/2 cup (75 g) golden raisins

2 tart apples, peeled, cored, and chopped

1 cup (123 g) shelled pistachio nuts

1 cup (140 g) chopped almonds

2/3 cup (160 ml) sweet red Passover wine

1/4 cup (60 ml) apple cider vinegar

2 teaspoons grated fresh orange peel

2 teaspoons chopped fresh ginger

3/4 teaspoon ground cinnamon

1/2 teaspoon cayenne pepper

1/2 cup (160 g) orange marmalade

TIP

Make this a day before serving to allow the flavors to blend and mellow. It may be made up to 3 days ahead. Store in the refrigerator, but remove from the refrigerator about 30 minutes before serving. Serve at room temperature.

Combine all the ingredients in a bowl, mix, and let rest on the countertop at least 4 hours before serving. Mix the ingredients occasionally during that time.

Yield: Makes 6 cups (1.5 kg)

SERVING SUGGESTIONS AND VARIATIONS: The peppery heat gives this haroset real vitality, but if you don't like spicy, hot food, you can leave out the cayenne pepper.

HONEY FRITTERS WITH RAISINS AND PINE NUTS

(P)

I can't imagine a Passover Seder without this dish. My grandmother made it with walnuts but I switched to pine nuts and that meant adding a few raisins and orange peel. Still—it is Grandma's recipe, isn't it?

3 large eggs, separated

Pinch of salt

1 tablespoon (15 ml) vegetable oil,
plus additional for frying

1 teaspoon grated fresh orange or lemon peel

1/4 cup (50 g) sugar

3/4 cup (87 g) matzo meal

Approximately 1 pound (455 g) honey

1/2 cup (75 g) raisins

1/3 cup (45 g) pine nuts

TIP

You can make these a day or so ahead, but remember that these fritters will absorb honey as they sit. I always add more honey as the days go by.

Beat the egg yolks, salt, and 1 tablespoon (15 ml) vegetable oil together in a bowl. Stir in the citrus peel and set aside. In a separate bowl, beat the egg whites and sugar until they are glossy and stand in stiff peaks. Fold into the yolk mixture. Fold in the matzo meal. Let stand for 30 minutes. With wet hands, shape a walnut-size ball of dough into a round about 1/2 inch (1.3 cm) thick. Heat about 1/4 inch (6 mm) vegetable oil in a sauté pan over medium heat. Fry the rounds for 1 to 2 minutes per side or until golden brown. Drain them on paper towels. Place the rounds in a saucepan. Pour the honey over them. Add the raisins and pine nuts. Cook over low heat for 5 to 6 minutes or until they are all coated and heated through. They may be served at this point, but they are better if they stand for several hours or 1 to 2 days and reheated. (These do not need refrigeration if you finish them within two days; after that I put them in the fridge.)

Yield: Makes 10 to 12 servings

SERVING SUGGESTIONS AND VARIATIONS: Make Grandma's original: 1 cup (120 g) chopped walnuts instead of the pine nuts, raisins, and orange peel.

STIR-FRIED QUINOA WITH MUSHROOMS AND SWISS CHARD

Ⓟ

There are so many reasons to love quinoa! For one thing, it's nutritious—a complete protein. Second, it's widely available, relatively cheap, and easy to cook. It's also versatile. You can make it into salad, casseroles, stuffings, and so on. It tastes good! What more can you ask? This: It's okay during Passover!

1 cup (173 g) quinoa

1½ cups (355 ml) water

5 tablespoons (75 ml) olive oil, divided

1 large onion, chopped

1 stalk celery, sliced into ½-inch (1.3-cm) pieces

2 cloves garlic, chopped

1 serrano (or other chile) pepper, deseeded and chopped

1 cup (70 g) chopped mushrooms

3 cups (about 4 ounces, or 115 g) chopped Swiss chard (or kale)

½ cup (120 ml) vegetable stock

3 tablespoons (45 ml) lemon juice

1 teaspoon grated lemon peel

Salt and freshly ground black pepper, to taste

Chopped cashews, optional

Place the quinoa in a strainer, rinse thoroughly with cold water, and drain. Bring the water to a boil, add the quinoa, and bring to a boil again. Stir and lower the heat; simmer, covered, for about 15 minutes, or until all the liquid has been absorbed and the grains are tender. Remove the pan from the heat and spoon the quinoa into a bowl to cool. Heat 3 tablespoons (45 ml) of the olive oil in a sauté pan over medium heat. Add the onion and celery and cook for 4 to 5 minutes or until lightly browned. Add the garlic and serrano pepper and cook for another 1 to 2 minutes. Add the mushrooms and chard, and cook, tossing the ingredients, for another minute. Add the stock and raise the heat to a simmer. Cook, stirring frequently, for 2 to 3 minutes or until the pan juices have evaporated. Add the quinoa, remaining olive oil, lemon juice, and lemon peel. Stir to distribute the ingredients evenly. Season with salt and pepper. Serve garnished with chopped cashews, if desired. Serve hot or at room temperature.

Yield: Makes 4 servings

DID YOU KNOW? Not everyone agrees that quinoa is permissible during Passover (please check with your rabbi). It is actually not a grain. It doesn't rise. But some quinoa may be grown near other prohibited grains, so it is among those products that must be labeled "kosher for Passover."

BRAISED CHICKEN WITH RHUBARB GRAVY

(M)

Rhubarb is in season about the same time as Passover. I usually stew it with some sugar and serve it, like cranberry sauce, with meat. But it also lends an interesting, piquant flavor to mild foods such as chicken.

1 broiler-fryer chicken, cut into 8 pieces

2 tablespoons (30 ml) olive oil

1 large shallot, chopped

2 tablespoons (12 g) finely chopped fresh ginger

1/2 cup (120 ml) chicken stock

1/2 cup (120 ml) orange juice

1/4 cup (80 g) honey

Salt and freshly ground black pepper, to taste

1 teaspoon grated fresh orange peel

1 pound (455 g) rhubarb stalks, cut into 1/2-inch (1.3-cm) chunks

Rinse and dry the chicken. Heat the olive oil in a deep sauté pan over medium heat and cook the chicken pieces a few at a time for 8 to 10 minutes or until lightly browned. Remove the chicken from the pan and discard all but a film of the pan fat. Add the shallot and ginger to the pan and cook for 1 to 2 minutes. Pour in the stock, juice, and honey. Bring the liquid to a boil and cook for 3 to 4 minutes to reduce it slightly. Return the chicken to the pan and sprinkle with salt, pepper, and orange peel. Cover the pan and simmer for about 20 minutes. Add the rhubarb and cook for another 5 to 10 minutes or until the chicken is completely cooked through. Remove the chicken from the pan and keep it warm. Raise the heat under the pan and cook the pan fluids for about 5 minutes, stirring often to break up chunks of rhubarb, or until the sauce has thickened to a gravy-like consistency. Serve the chicken with the gravy.

Yield: Makes 4 servings

DID YOU KNOW? Rhubarb leaves are poisonous, which is why you can only buy the stalks in the store. If you grow your own rhubarb, discard the leaves.

BRAISED LAMB SHOULDER ROAST WITH CHOCOLATE

(M)

The chocolate adds a beautiful, rich, dark sheen to the gravy.

2 tablespoons (30 ml) olive oil

1 shoulder of lamb roast, 3½ to 4 pounds (1.6 to 1.8 kg)

2 medium onions, chopped

3 carrots, chopped

1¼ cups (295 ml) white wine

1¼ cups (295 ml) chicken stock

1 cup (245 g) tomato sauce

¼ cup (15 g) chopped fresh parsley

1 teaspoon fresh thyme leaves

1 bay leaf

¼ teaspoon ground cinnamon

2 strips of orange peel, each about 2 inches (5 cm) long

1 ounce (28 g) unsweetened chocolate

Salt and freshly ground black pepper, to taste

Preheat the oven to 300°F (150°C, or gas mark 2). Heat the olive oil in a deep heat-proof casserole. Add the roast and cook over medium heat, turning it occasionally, for 8 to 10 minutes or until lightly browned. Remove the meat and set aside. Add the onions and carrots to the pan and cook for 3 to 4 minutes or until they have softened. Pour in the wine, stock, and tomato sauce and mix the ingredients. Add the parsley, thyme, bay leaf, cinnamon, orange peel, chocolate, salt, and pepper. Stir the ingredients until the chocolate has melted. Return the roast to the pan. Cover the pan. Bake for about 2½ to 3 hours, turning the meat occasionally, or until the meat is tender. Discard the bay leaf and orange peel. Remove the meat and let it rest for several minutes before carving. Skim the fat from the top of the pan fluids. Serve the pan fluids and vegetables with the meat. Or boil the pan fluids (with the vegetables) for a few minutes, if desired, for thicker gravy.

Yield: Makes 4 to 6 servings

SERVING SUGGESTIONS AND VARIATIONS: You can make this dish using 4 meaty lamb shanks.

DID YOU KNOW? It was an ancient custom to sacrifice a lamb before Passover and then eat it to begin the festival. That custom ended with the destruction of the Temple in 70 A.D. Since that time, out of respect, we don't eat roasted lamb during Passover. Some people will not eat roasted meat of any kind. But lamb itself is not forbidden if it is braised with liquid as in this recipe.

"POLENTA" CRISPS

Ⓜ

We always have so much food left over after the Seders that it can take several days to use all of it up. The usual salads can get tiresome, so one year I made mock polenta—using matzo meal instead of cornmeal. It was a big hit, so I created other versions, some with cheese, some with vegetables. This one includes leftover chicken or turkey and what's left of the traditional Seder chicken soup (carrot, parsnip, and stock).

2 tablespoons (30 ml) vegetable oil, plus additional for frying

1/2 cup (52 g) chopped leek, white part only

1 cup (80 g) finely chopped mushrooms

1 cooked carrot, chopped

1 cooked parsnip, chopped

3 cups (710 ml) chicken or vegetable stock

1 cup (120 g) matzo meal

1 cup (140 g) chopped cooked chicken or turkey

2 tablespoons (8 g) chopped fresh dill

Salt and freshly ground black pepper, to taste

Lightly grease a 9 x 5 x 3-inch (23 x 13 x 7.5-cm) or 8½ x 4½ x 2½-inch (21.5 x 11.5 x 6.5-cm) loaf pan. Heat 2 tablespoons (30 ml) vegetable oil in a sauté pan over medium heat. Add the leek and mushrooms and cook, stirring occasionally, for 3 to 4 minutes or until the liquid has evaporated from the pan. Set aside to cool slightly. Mix in the carrot and parsnip. Bring the stock to a boil in a large saucepan. Whisk constantly as you gradually add the matzo meal and cook for about 2 minutes or until the mixture has thickened. Reduce the heat to low and let the mixture simmer, stirring occasionally, for 3 to 4 minutes or until very thick. Stir in the chicken or turkey, vegetable mixture, and dill; season with salt and pepper. Spoon the mixture into the prepared pan. Refrigerate until cold and firm, at least 1 hour. Unmold the polenta and cut it into 3/4-inch (2-cm) slices. Heat some vegetable oil in a sauté pan over medium heat and cook the slices for 2 to 4 minutes per side or until browned and crispy.

Yield: Makes 6 servings

SERVING SUGGESTIONS AND VARIATIONS: You can make these crisps with leftover brisket and use some of the pan juices instead of or in addition to stock. This dish is a good bet for lunch, but for dinner you could serve the crisps with sunny-side up eggs and/or roasted vegetables.

JAM FINGERS

Flourless jelly rolls are popular for Passover, and I've served them on numerous holidays. I sometimes cut them in a variety of ways instead of rolling them, like making them into mini cakes such as these.

6 large eggs, separated

1/2 cup (100 g) sugar, divided

Pinch of salt

1 1/2 cups (143 g) ground pistachios

2 teaspoons grated orange peel

1/2 teaspoon ground cinnamon

Potato starch or Passover confectioners' sugar

3/4 cup (240 g) apricot jam

1 tablespoon (20 g) apricot or orange juice

Passover confectioners' sugar

Preheat the oven to 350°F (180°C, or gas mark 4). Line a 15 1/2 x 10 1/2-inch (39.5 x 27-cm) jelly-roll pan with parchment paper and lightly oil the paper. Set aside. Beat the egg yolks with 6 tablespoons (78 g) sugar and the salt in an electric mixer set at medium for 3 to 5 minutes or until the mixture is thick and pale. Stir in the pistachios, orange peel, and cinnamon. Spoon the mixture into a bowl and set aside. Clean the mixing bowl and add the egg whites. Beat the egg whites with a wire whisk attachment at medium speed until they are foamy. While continuously beating, gradually add the remaining sugar and beat until the whites stand in stiff peaks. Add one-third of the whites into the yolk-nut mixture and blend in thoroughly. Add the remaining beaten whites and fold them in gently. Spread the batter evenly in the prepared pan. Bake for 18 to 20 minutes or until the cake is lightly browned and springs back when touched gently. Use a knife to loosen the edges of the cake around the sides of the pan. Place a kitchen towel or large board on a clean work surface and sprinkle it lightly with potato starch or Passover confectioners' sugar. Invert the cake over the towel or board and pat the pan to loosen the cake. Remove the parchment paper. Cover the cake with plastic wrap. Let cool. When the cake is cool, cut it in half, to make two pieces about 7 3/4 x 10 1/2-inches (20 x 27-cm). Mix the jam and juice and spread on top of one of the halves, leaving a small (about 1/2-inch [1.3-cm]) border. Place the second half on top of the jam. Trim the border. Cut the cake into 6 sections on the wider side, 4 sections on the longer side, creating 24 pieces. Dust the tops with confectioners' sugar.

Yield: Makes 24 pieces

SERVING SUGGESTIONS AND VARIATIONS: Serve this the standard way: Invert the cake onto a towel, roll the towel, and let the cake cool. After you unroll the cooled cake and spread it with the jam, roll it again. Dust the top with confectioners' sugar.

BABY FUDGE CAKES

(P)

These are ultra-rich and chocolaty.

Raspberry Sauce, optional (see sidebar for recipe)

1/4 cup (56 g) Passover margarine

1/4 cup (56 g) coconut oil

5 ounces (140 g) bittersweet chocolate, chopped

3 large eggs

1/2 cup (43 g) unsweetened cocoa powder

3/4 cup (150 g) sugar

1 teaspoon vanilla extract

Passover confectioners' sugar and crushed candied ginger, optional

Raspberry Sauce:

2 cups (250 g) fresh raspberries

3 tablespoons (40 g) sugar

2 tablespoons (30 ml) orange flavored liqueur or orange juice

Place the berries, sugar, and liqueur in a blender or food processor and purée for a minute until the ingredients are well combined. Strain if desired. Makes about 1 1/2 cups (450 g).

Make the Raspberry Sauce, if desired. Set aside. Preheat the oven to 300°F (150°C, or gas mark 2). Generously grease 12 muffin tin cups, preferably nonstick. Place the margarine, coconut oil, and chocolate in the top part of a double boiler over barely simmering water. Stir until the chocolate has melted and the mixture is uniform. Remove the top part of the pan from the heat and set it aside to cool. In the bowl of an electric mixer, beat the eggs for about 1 minute at medium speed, until well blended. Add the cocoa and beat it in thoroughly. Gradually add the sugar and continue to beat for about 3 minutes, or until all the sugar has been incorporated and the mixture is thick. Add the chocolate mixture and vanilla extract and beat them in thoroughly. Spoon equal amounts of the batter into the prepared muffin tins. Place the muffin tin in a bain-marie. Bake for about 45 minutes, or until the cakes are set and have risen slightly (they may look slightly broken on top). Remove the muffin tin from the bain-marie. Place the muffin tin back in the oven without the bain-marie. Bake for 5 minutes. Remove the pan from the oven and let cool for 5 minutes. Invert the pan over a cake rack. Let the cakes cool upside down on the rack. Once cool, use a knife to loosen the edges of the cakes around the sides of the cups. Shake out the cakes. Serve the cakes with the Raspberry Sauce and sprinkled with Passover confectioners' sugar or crushed crystallized ginger, if desired.

Yield: Makes 12 cakes

SERVING SUGGESTIONS AND VARIATIONS: For a dairy meal you can serve these cakes with whipped cream or the Roasted Strawberry Balsamic Ice Cream on page 179.

NOT MY GRANDMA'S KUMPUT

(P)

On Passover and for the Jewish High Holidays, my grandma served what she called kumput, *made with stewed prunes and dried apricots. But when I was in Egypt I tasted a dish that looked like kumput but it was actually a dish called* khoshaf, *a Muslim specialty (often served to break the Ramadan fast). Unlike Grandma's kumput, khoshaf isn't stewed or cooked at all, so the fruit stays firm and pleasantly chewy after soaking in hot, sweet syrup. Frankly, it's much better than Grandma's dish and I serve it during Passover in her memory, even though it isn't her recipe.*

1 1/2 cups (355 ml) water

1 cup (235 ml) mango or apricot juice

3 tablespoons (60 g) honey

1 teaspoon vanilla extract

1 cup (175 g) cut-up prunes

1 cup (175 g) cut-up dried apricots

1 cup (150 g) golden raisins

1 cup (175 g) cut-up dried figs or dates

2 tablespoons (28 g) crushed crystallized ginger

Chopped toasted almonds or pistachios

Combine the water, mango juice, and honey in a saucepan. Bring to a boil over high heat, stir, and cook for 4 to 5 minutes, or until syrupy. Remove the pan from the heat, let cool slightly, and stir in the vanilla extract. Place the prunes, apricots, raisins, figs, and ginger in a bowl. Pour the syrup over the fruit. Toss to coat all the fruit with the syrup. Let marinate for at least 1 hour. Serve sprinkled with the nuts.

Yield: Makes 6 servings

SERVING SUGGESTIONS AND VARIATIONS: Although kumput is meant to be served as is, it's also good with sorbet or ice cream.

ROASTED STRAWBERRY BALSAMIC ICE CREAM

(D)

You can find strawberries throughout the year, but the best ones—the smaller, local berries—start their season at about the same time as Passover, which make them a natural for holiday desserts. Roasting strawberries intensifies their fruit sugar flavor, and that, plus the small amount of balsamic vinegar in this recipe, makes this more than the usual strawberry ice cream.

2 pints (about 1 pound, or 455 g) strawberries

3/4 cup (150 g) sugar, divided

1 teaspoon grated fresh orange peel

3 cups (710 ml) half-and-half, light cream, or whipping cream, divided

3 large egg yolks

1/8 teaspoon salt

2 tablespoons (30 ml) balsamic vinegar

TIP

The strawberries give off a lot of juices as they roast. Using a jelly-roll pan prevents the juices from dripping into your oven.

Preheat the oven to 300°F (150°C, or gas mark 2). Line a jelly-roll pan with parchment paper. Rinse the berries and remove the stems. Place the berries on top of the parchment paper. Sprinkle with 2 tablespoons (26 g) sugar and the orange peel. Toss the berries to coat them evenly. Roast for about 35 to 40 minutes or until very soft. Remove the pan from the oven and crush the berries with a fork. Set aside to cool. While the strawberries are roasting, heat 2 cups (475 ml) cream over medium heat until bubbles appear around the edges of the pan. Set aside. In the bowl of an electric mixer, beat the remaining sugar, the egg yolks, and salt at medium speed for 3 to 5 minutes or until light and thick. Gradually add the heated cream and mix the ingredients until the mixture is uniform in color. Return the mixture to the saucepan and cook over medium heat, stirring constantly, for 5 to 6 minutes or until thickened enough to coat the back of a spoon. Pour in the remaining cream and blend it in thoroughly. Place the mixture in the refrigerator until thoroughly chilled. Stir in the balsamic vinegar and the strawberry mixture, including all the accumulated juices. Freeze in an ice cream freezer according to manufacturer's directions.

Yield: Makes about 1 quart (946 ml)

chapter

12

DESSERTS

How many times have you thought about what to make for dinner backwards—that is, dessert first? Or been in a restaurant and looked at the dessert menu first? Why not! Most of us like to save room for the sweet treat, which can mean anything from the humblest, homey Baked Apples with Ginger and Orange to the most elegant Roasted Pears with Honey Crème Fraîche and Lime.

BAKED APPLES WITH GINGER AND ORANGE

(P)

We are an apple-eating family. I grew up with a mom who baked the best apple pies ever, and Ed's mom was the queen of the baked apple. I make both of these desserts every autumn, after I shop at a local orchard and buy different kinds of apples for each. I make my apple pies the same way, every year, every time. But baked apples are a different story. I don't think I ever make the same recipe twice because what I make depends on what ingredients I happen to have on hand and my mood. The recipe is so versatile you can change it in a zillion ways to suit your own tastes.

4 large baking apples

Half of 1 lemon

6 tablespoons (54 g) golden raisins

2 tablespoons (18 g) chopped toasted almonds

2 teaspoons (4g) grated fresh orange peel

2 teaspoons (6g) crushed crystallized ginger

1/4 teaspoon ground cinnamon

1/4 cup (80 g) honey, divided

1 cup (235 ml) apple cider or any kind of fruit juice, divided

1 tablespoon (14 g) coconut oil or Earth Balance Buttery Spread, cut into 4 pieces

Preheat the oven to 375°F (190°C, or gas mark 5). Wash the apples and remove the seeds and cores, leaving about 1/2 inch (1.3 cm) at the bottom. Peel the apples about halfway down from the top. Rub the cut surfaces with the cut side of the lemon. Place the apples in a baking dish. Mix the raisins, almonds, orange peel, ginger, cinnamon, 2 tablespoons (40 g) honey, and 3 tablespoons (45 ml) cider or juice in a small bowl. Spoon equal amounts of this mixture into the hollowed apple cores. Combine the remaining honey and juice and pour over the apples. Dot the tops with the coconut oil or Earth Balance Buttery Spread. Bake for 45 minutes, or until the apples are tender, basting occasionally with the pan juices.

Yield: Makes 4 servings

DID YOU KNOW? The best apple varieties for baked apples are Cortland and Rome Beauty, but you can use Gala, Jonagold, or Golden Delicious, too.

FUDGE AND RUM CUSTARD PIE

(D)

I daydream about this pie. Because the firm and flaky crust is such a brilliant contrast with the soft center, I love how it feels on my tongue. And then there's the mix of flavors: rich chocolate, spicy rum, and fluffy whipped cream! It looks festive, too. I've made this for family, but it's definitely for company, too.

1 unbaked 9-inch (23-cm) pie crust

1 envelope unflavored gelatin

1/4 cup (60 ml) water

3/4 cup (150 g) sugar, divided

1 tablespoon (8 g) cornstarch

Pinch of salt

2 cups (475 ml) milk

4 large egg yolks

2 ounces (55 g) unsweetened chocolate, chopped

1 teaspoon vanilla extract

3 tablespoons (45 ml) rum, preferably dark rum

1 1/2 cups (355 ml) whipping cream

Chopped pecans, cocoa powder,

or shaved chocolate

TIP

If the rum custard is too cold and thick to mix with the whipped cream, use a whisk to soften and smooth it.

Bake the crust (see tip) and set it aside. Mix the gelatin and water in a small bowl and set it aside.

Combine 1/2 cup (100 g) sugar, the cornstarch, salt, and milk in the top part of a double boiler set over simmering water. Cook, whisking frequently, for about 10 minutes, or until thickened. Add the egg yolks and cook for 3 to 4 minutes. Don't let mixture come to a boil. Add the gelatin mixture. Stir until completely dissolved. Cook the mixture for 8 to 10 minutes, or until thick enough to coat the back of a spoon.

Mix 1 cup (230 g) of this custard with the chocolate and the vanilla extract. Stir to blend completely. Spoon the mixture into the baked pie crust; place in the refrigerator to chill. Add the rum to the remaining custard and refrigerate the mixture until it has cooled.

Beat the whipping cream with the remaining 1/4 cup (50 g) sugar until thick. Mix one-third of the whipped cream with the rum-custard mixture. Spoon this rum mixture over the chocolate layer. Spread the remaining whipped cream on top of rum custard.

Garnish with chopped pecans, or dust with cocoa powder or shaved chocolate.

Yield: Makes one 9-inch (23-cm) pie, or 8 servings

DID YOU KNOW? "Thick enough to coat the back of a spoon" means that when you immerse a spoon in the mixture and swipe the back with your finger, it will form a permanent line. If a lot of the liquid drips down into the line, the mixture needs more cooking.

TIP

To bake the pie crust, preheat the oven to 400°F (200°C, or gas mark 6). After fitting the crust into the pie pan, prick the dough with the tines of a fork, cover it with aluminum foil and place pie weights or dry beans on top of the foil. Bake for 10 minutes. Remove the weights and foil, prick the dough again, return the pie to the oven and bake for another 10 minutes or until the crust is golden brown.

HI-HAT LEMON YOGURT CUPCAKES WITH LEMON CREAM CHEESE FROSTING

(D)

These cupcakes are rich, with a dense texture. But because I don't like desserts that are cloyingly sweet, I've cut down substantially on the amount of confectioners' sugar in the frosting to about half of what standard recipes call for. It's much better because you can taste the other ingredients—butter and cheese, a spike of lemon—not just sugar.

For the Hi-Hat Lemon Yogurt Cupcakes:

1½ cups (187 g) all-purpose flour

2 teaspoons baking powder

½ teaspoon salt

1 cup (200 g) sugar

¼ cup (60 ml) vegetable oil

3 large eggs

1 cup (230 g) plain yogurt

Grated peel of 1 large lemon

Juice of 1 large lemon

For the Lemon Cream Cheese Frosting:

8 ounces (225 g) cream cheese, softened

4 tablespoons (56 g) butter

½ teaspoon vanilla extract

1½ cups (180 g) confectioners' sugar

1½ teaspoons (3g) grated fresh lemon peel

1 teaspoon lemon juice

> **TIP**
> These freeze well; wrap them individually in plastic wrap or in a single layer in a covered container.

Make the Hi-Hat Lemon Yogurt Cupcakes: Preheat the oven to 350°F (180°C, or gas mark 4). Lightly grease 12 muffin tin cups. In a bowl, mix together the flour, baking powder, and salt. Set aside. In another bowl beat the sugar and vegetable oil together at medium speed until well blended. Add the eggs, one at a time, beating after each addition. Add the yogurt, lemon peel, and lemon juice. Beat until well blended. Add the dry ingredients and beat them in. Spoon equal amounts of the batter into the prepared pan. Bake for about 20 minutes or until a cake tester inserted into the center comes out clean. Remove to a rack to cool. Frost with Lemon Cream Cheese Frosting.

Make the Lemon Cream Cheese Frosting: Beat the cream cheese, butter, vanilla extract, confectioners' sugar, lemon peel, and lemon juice until well blended and spreadable. Makes about 1¾ cups (370 g).

Yield: Makes 12 cupcakes

POACHED FIGS WITH HONEY, ORANGE, AND SPICES

Figs are a wonderful breakfast or brunch treat. But dressed up with reduced syrup, a mysterious hint of spices and pepper, and a dusting of crushed almonds, they are pretty enough for dessert, too, and especially welcome after a heavy meal. Serve them plain or with ice cream or sorbet.

1 cup (235 ml) sweet white wine	6 whole black peppercorns
1 cup (235 ml) water	2 strips orange peel, 2 inches (5 cm) long
1/2 cup (160 g) honey	8 large fresh figs
4 green cardamom pods, slightly crushed	1 to 2 tablespoons (10 to 20 g) crushed
6 allspice berries or clover	toasted almonds

Combine the wine, water, honey, cardamom pods, allspice berries, peppercorns, and orange peel in a saucepan over medium-high heat. Bring the liquid to a boil, reduce the heat to a simmer, and cook for 15 minutes. Add the figs and simmer for about 10 minutes or until the fruit is tender but not soft or mushy. Remove the pan from the heat, remove the figs to a dish, and let cool. Strain the liquid (discard the cardamom, allspice, peppercorns, and orange peel) and pour the strained liquid back into the pan. Boil the liquid over high heat until it is syrupy. Let the syrup cool. Cut the figs into quarters and place 8 pieces on each of 4 dessert dishes. Drizzle with syrup and sprinkle with the nuts. (If the syrup has firmed, heat it for a minute or so over medium heat to liquefy.)

Yield: Makes 4 servings

SUBSTITUTIONS AND VARIATIONS: Use this poaching fluid for several other kinds of fruit such as peaches, nectarines, and plums.

DID YOU KNOW? There are two types of cardamom: green and black. The black has a smoky flavor and so is a better choice for savory dishes. Although cardamom is popular in Indian cuisine, you can find it everywhere in supermarkets

SAINT CUPCAKE BROWNIE COOKIES (D)

One of my favorite blogs is www.Sprinklefingers.com, written by Jami Curl, queen of cakes and confections in Portland, Oregon. She owns and operates two bakeries (Saint Cupcake) plus a candy and confectionary palace (Quin). These cookies, posted to her site, are not to be missed. I changed the ingredient list measurements and instructions for easy home use, but they are Jami's cookies and they are awesome. Plain is fine. Or dunked. Or used as sandwich outsides with ice cream in the middle.

4 tablespoons (56 g) butter, cut into small pieces

12 ounces (340 g) semisweet chocolate

1/3 cup (42 g) all-purpose flour

1/4 teaspoon salt

1/4 teaspoon baking powder

2 large eggs plus 1 large egg yolk

1/2 cup (100 g) sugar

1/4 cup (60 g) packed brown sugar

1 tablespoon (15 ml) vanilla extract

Preheat the oven to 350°F (180°C, or gas mark 4). Line a cookie sheet with parchment paper (or grease the cookie sheet lightly). Melt the butter and chocolate together in the top part of a double boiler over simmering water. Remove the pan from the heat, mix the ingredients to blend them thoroughly, and set aside to cool. Sift the flour, salt, and baking powder together in a bowl and set aside. Beat the eggs, egg yolk, sugar, brown sugar, and vanilla extract in the bowl of an electric mixer set at medium speed, until well blended, about 3 to 5 minutes. Fold the cooled chocolate mixture into the egg mixture until thoroughly blended. Add the flour mixture and blend it in thoroughly. Let the batter rest for 20 minutes or until thick enough to scoop. Use a 2 ounce (55 g) scoop to form a rounded mound and place the dough on the prepared cookie sheet. Leave space between the cookies for expansion. Bake for 15 to 17 minutes. Alternatively, use a 1 ounce (27 g) scoop to make smaller cookies and bake for 10 to 12 minutes. Cookies should be cracked, with moist looking ingredients inside the cracks.

Yield: Makes 12 or 24 cookies

HONEY CASHEW-CRANBERRY PIE

(P)

I invented this pie out of necessity because we all love pecan pie in my family, but my daughter Gillian is allergic to pecans. Substituting isn't that difficult except that nut textures and flavors are so different from one another. Cashews are soft, like pecans, so they're a good choice with the soft sugar custard in this pie. But they need a different sweetener than the usual corn syrup, so I switched to honey. I added the fresh orange peel and cranberries to give a tangy finish to this rather sweet confection.

2/3 cup (230 g) honey

1/3 cup (67 g) sugar

3 large eggs

3 tablespoons (42 g) Earth Balance Buttery Spread or margarine, melted

1½ tablespoons (12 g) all-purpose flour

2 teaspoons (4 g) grated fresh orange peel

1/4 teaspoon salt

1 teaspoon vanilla extract

1 cup (110 g) chopped fresh cranberries

1 cup (145 g) chopped cashews

1 unbaked 9-inch (23-cm) pie crust

TIP

Cranberries freeze well for up to 1 year. In the autumn, buy 2 to 3 bags when you see them in the market, so you can cook with them throughout the year.

Preheat the oven the 350°F (180°C, or gas mark 4). Combine the honey, sugar, eggs, and melted spread or margarine in a bowl and whisk the ingredients until well blended. Stir in the flour, orange peel, salt, and vanilla extract and blend them in thoroughly. Stir in the cranberries and cashews. Pour the mixture into the pie crust. Bake for about 45 minutes or until the top is richly brown and crunchy.

Yield: Makes one 9-inch (23-cm) pie, or 8 servings

ORANGE ALASKAS

(P)

This is a beautiful way to serve fresh fruit and it is particularly refreshing after a big or heavy meal. Consider this dessert at Passover! Serve one or two halves to each person.

6 navel oranges

12 strawberries, halved or quartered

24 seedless red grapes, halved

1/2 cup (100 g) plus 6 tablespoons (78 g) sugar, divided

1/4 cup (60 ml) orange flavored liqueur, brandy, or orange juice

3 large egg whites

TIP

Cut and carve the oranges ahead by a day and refrigerate; use all the juices that may accumulate in addition to the brandy.

Cut the oranges in half, carve out the flesh and cut the flesh into bite-size pieces. Place the flesh in a bowl and add the strawberries, grapes, 6 tablespoons (78 g) sugar, and liqueur. Toss the fruit and let soak for at least 1 hour. Preheat the oven to 425°F (220°C, or gas mark 7). Cut a tiny slice from the bottom of each orange half so that they will sit upright on a plate. Spoon the fruit and accumulated juices back into the reserved orange halves. Set aside. Beat the egg whites until foamy. Gradually add the remaining 1/2 cup (100 g) sugar, beating constantly until the whites stand in stiff, glossy peaks. Spread the meringue over the top of the orange halves, mounding it in the center and making sure to seal the edges to the fruit. Place the filled oranges on a cookie sheet. Bake for about 6 minutes or until the meringue is lightly browned. Let cool slightly and serve.

Yield: Makes 6 to 12 servings

SERVING SUGGESTIONS AND VARIATIONS: You can add or substitute any fresh colorful fruit such as kiwi, blueberries, or raspberries.

MARY TODD LINCOLN COURTIN' CAKE Ⓓ

I was inspired to make this old-fashioned cake after I saw the movie Lincoln. *Supposedly, Mary Todd Lincoln made this for Abe while they were dating. He liked it so much that it sealed the deal and he proposed marriage to her. It's probably not true, but does it really matter? The cake is legendary because it is so light and tender, and it's beautiful, too. It's simply wonderful as is, but if you're in an indulgent sort of mood, serve it with homemade Roasted Strawberry Balsamic Ice Cream (page 179).*

2¼ cups (281 g) cake flour

1 tablespoon (15 g) baking powder

½ teaspoon salt

1 cup (150 g) ground almonds

1 cup (225 g) butter, softened

1½ cups (300 g) sugar

1 cup (235 ml) whole milk

1 tablespoon (15 ml) vanilla extract

6 large egg whites

Confectioners' sugar, for decorating

TIP

Separate the eggs first, because it's easier to do when they are cold (use the yolks for another recipe). The whites whip to the greatest volume when they're at room temperature, so they'll be ready by the time you prepare everything else for this recipe.

Preheat the oven to 350°F (180°C, or gas mark 4). Lightly grease and flour a 10 cup (2.4 L) Bundt pan and set aside. Sift the flour, baking powder, and salt into a bowl. Sift these ingredients another two times. Mix in the ground almonds and set aside. Place the butter and sugar in the bowl of an electric mixer and beat at medium speed for 1 to 2 minutes or until smooth and creamy. Gradually add the flour mixture, alternating with the milk, beating after each addition until the mixture is smooth and uniform. Stir in the vanilla extract. In a separate bowl, beat the egg whites until they stand in stiff, glossy peaks. Fold the whites into the batter. Spoon the batter into the prepared pan. Bake for about 1 hour or until a cake tester inserted into the center comes out clean. Remove from the oven to a cake rack and cool for 10 minutes. Invert onto the cake rack to cool completely. Decorate with sifted confectioners' sugar.

Yield: Makes 1 cake, or 12 servings

LEMON OATMEAL COOKIES

(D)

Our local Hadassah chapter holds a biweekly Afternoon Tea for cancer patients and their caregivers at Stamford Hospital, and I am one of the "regular" bakers. These buttery cookies are eggless, ultra-tender, and light as air and always get a thumbs-up, so I've sent them several times.

1 pound (455 g) butter, softened

1 cup (200 g) sugar

2 cups (250 g) all-purpose flour

1/2 teaspoon salt

3 cups (240 g) quick oats

1 tablespoon (6 g) grated fresh lemon peel

1 teaspoon vanilla extract

Confectioners' sugar

TIP

These freeze well; place them in plastic-covered containers. You can eat these straight from the freezer.

Preheat the oven to 350°F (180°C, or gas mark 4). Beat the butter and sugar in the bowl of an electric mixer set at medium speed for 2 to 3 minutes or until well blended. Add the flour, salt, oats, lemon peel, and vanilla extract and mix to blend ingredients thoroughly. Chill the dough for at least 30 minutes. Remove small portions of the dough and shape the pieces into 1-inch (2.5-cm) balls. Place the balls on an ungreased cookie sheet, leaving some space between them. Spoon a film of confectioners' sugar onto a dish. Press the bottom of a drinking tumbler into the sugar. Press the balls flat with the bottom of the sugared tumbler. Repeat until all the cookies are flat. Bake for about 15 minutes or until lightly browned. Let cool for 10 minutes on the cookie sheet, then remove to a rack to cool completely.

Yield: Makes about 100 cookies

ROASTED PEARS WITH HONEY CRÈME FRAÎCHE AND LIME

(D)

This sophisticated dessert looks as if you've fussed, but it is incredibly easy to cook—more or less like baked apples. And, as with baked apples, you can eat the fruit plain, but that extra indulgence of sweetened cream and the lime peel tang bring it all together.

2 large ripe Bartlett pears, peeled

Half of 1 lemon

2 tablespoons (30 ml) mango or apple juice

1 tablespoon (14 g) butter, melted

1 teaspoon vanilla extract, divided

2 teaspoons (9 g) sugar

6 ounces (170 g) crème fraîche

1 tablespoon (20 g) honey

1 teaspoon finely grated fresh lime peel

TIP

Use pears that are ripe and have a little "give" when you press them with your fingers. Rock-hard pears won't bake properly and overripe pears will be too mushy.

Preheat the oven to 400°F (200°C, or gas mark 6). Cut the pears in half and remove the inner core and seeds. Rub the surface with the cut half of a lemon. Place the pear halves in a baking dish just large enough to hold them so they don't tip over. Mix the mango juice, melted butter, and 1/2 teaspoon vanilla extract and spoon over the pears. Sprinkle the pears with the sugar. Roast for 15 minutes, baste with the pan juices, and roast another 12 to 15 minutes or until the pears are soft. Remove the pears and let them cool. When ready to serve, place the crème fraîche, honey, and remaining 1/2 teaspoon vanilla extract in a bowl and beat with an electric mixer set at medium speed for 1 to 2 minutes or until the crème fraîche is thick. Place 1 pear half in each of 4 dessert dishes. Spoon equal amounts of the crème fraîche into the pear hollows. Garnish with the lime peel and serve.

Yield: Makes 4 servings

SERVING SUGGESTIONS AND VARIATIONS: You can use yogurt, dairy sour cream, or sweetened whipped cream instead of crème fraîche. Bartletts are the best pears for baking because they are moderately sweet and hold up nicely in the oven heat, but you can use any large pear (Comice, Anjou, Bosc).

PRUNE PLUM CRISP

These days it's easy to buy almost any produce any time of year. But there are still some that are absolutely seasonal, such as Italian prune plums. Because they are only available for short time around August and September, they are that much more special. Grab them while you can! They are perfect for baking and few desserts are easier than this one.

3 pounds (1.4 kg) Italian prune plums

1/2 cup (100 g) sugar

3/4 teaspoon ground cinnamon, divided

1 tablespoon (15 ml) lemon juice

1/2 cup (64 g) plus 2 tablespoons (16 g) all-purpose flour, divided

1/4 cup (75 g) brown sugar

4 tablespoons (56 g) very cold Earth Balance Buttery Spread, cut into chunks

1/2 cup (78 g) old-fashioned oats

1/3 cup (47 g) chopped toasted almonds

Preheat the oven to 350°F (180°C, or gas mark 4). Wash and halve the plums and remove the pits. Cut the plum halves in half again. Combine the plums with the sugar, 1/2 teaspoon cinnamon, and lemon juice and mix well. Stir in 2 tablespoons (16 g) flour, and place the fruit mixture into a baking dish. Set aside. Place the remaining 1/2 cup (64 g) flour, brown sugar, remaining 1/4 teaspoon cinnamon, and Earth Balance Buttery Spread in the bowl of a food processor and process on pulse until the mixture resembles coarse crumbs. Add the oats and almonds and pulse briefly to incorporate them evenly. Spoon the mixture over the fruit. Bake for about 35 minutes or until the crust is crispy and golden brown.

Yield: Makes 6 servings

SUBSTITUTIONS AND VARIATIONS: Although prune plums have the perfect texture and moisture content for crisps and cobblers, you can use any type of plum. The crust is also ideal for crisps using other kinds of fruit.

DID YOU KNOW? Italian plums, President plums, and Empress plums are all similar, autumn varieties. Any of these will work for this crisp.

HONEY ROASTED FRUIT COCKTAIL Ⓟ

While I was growing up, my mom, Ed's mom, and everyone else's mom served canned fruit cocktail for dessert. All the kids wanted the maraschino cherries, which at some future time were discovered to get their bright color from carcinogenic red dye #2. Although canned fruit cocktail (now minus that dye) conjures lots of good memories, these days we prefer the homemade kind.

1/2 cup (120 ml) mango juice

2 tablespoons (40 g) honey

1 large, ripe mango, peeled and cut into bite-size chunks

2 large ripe pears, peeled, cored, and cut into bite-size chunks

1 cup (150 g) seedless red grapes

1 kiwi fruit, peeled and cut into bite-size chunks

16 to 18 strawberries, hulled

Ground cinnamon

1/4 cup (24 g) chopped fresh mint

Sorbet or ice cream, optional

Preheat the oven to 450°F (230°C, or gas mark 8). Line a jelly-roll sheet with parchment paper. Place the mango juice and honey in a saucepan and bring to a boil over high heat. Lower the heat and simmer for 3 to 4 minutes or until the liquid is slightly thickened. Set aside. Place the mango chunks, pear chunks, grapes, and kiwi chunks in a bowl. If the strawberries are large, cut them into pieces and add to the bowl; otherwise, add them whole. Pour the mango juice liquid over the fruit and toss to coat all the pieces. Spoon the fruit and liquid onto the parchment paper–lined pan. Sprinkle with cinnamon. Roast for 5 minutes. Toss the fruit around somewhat and roast for another 6 to 8 minutes or until fruit is soft and lightly caramelized. Remove the pan from the oven and let the fruit cool. Sprinkle with the mint. Place the fruit mixture and pan juices into serving dishes. Serve plain or with sorbet.

Yield: Makes 8 servings

SUBSTITUTIONS AND VARIATIONS: I've made this dish using many different fruits, including fresh pineapple chunks (roast the pieces an extra 3 to 4 minutes), apples, peaches, and blueberries (add them to the roasting pan for the last 3 to 4 minutes). You can switch juices, too, to orange, tangerine, or apple juice.

DID YOU KNOW? Roasting fruit intensifies their natural sugars so you don't need much additional sweetener.

SNOWCAP CHEESECAKE

Many years ago I was one of the judges of a cheesecake contest at a local cookware shop. I took tiny tastes of all of the cakes, and although many cakes were very good, only 3 were exceptional, including this one. I've changed the proportions and baking instructions over the years to suit my family's tastes. This dessert is rich and gorgeous, perfect for any festive occasion.

1 dozen chocolate graham crackers	4 large eggs
5 tablespoons (70 g) butter, melted	1 cup (230 g) dairy sour cream
8 ounces (225 g) bittersweet chocolate	1½ teaspoons (6 g) vanilla extract
1½ pounds (680 g) cream cheese, softened	2 cups (460 g) dairy sour cream
1 cup (200 g) sugar, divided	

Preheat the oven to 350°F (180°C, or gas mark 4). Butter a 9-inch (23-cm) springform pan. Crush the graham crackers and pulse them in a food processor until they resemble bread crumbs. Combine the crumbs with the melted butter and press onto the bottom and the lower part of the sides of the spring-form pan. Bake the crust for 10 minutes, remove it from the oven, and set aside. Melt the chocolate in the top part of a double boiler set over barely simmering water. When the chocolate has melted, remove the top part of the pan from the heat and let the chocolate cool. Beat the cream cheese and 3/4 cup (150 g) sugar together in an electric mixer set at medium for 3 to 4 minutes or until light and fluffy. Add the eggs, one at a time, beating after each addition. Stir in the 1 cup (230 g) sour cream and the vanilla extract until well blended. Divide the batter in half. Add the melted chocolate to one half and stir until well blended. Spoon the chocolate batter into the crust. Gently spoon the vanilla batter on top. Place the springform pan in a bain-marie. Bake for 55 to 60 minutes or until set. While the cake is in the oven, stir the sour cream and remaining 1/4 cup (50 g) sugar together to make the snowcap. After the cake has finished baking, remove it from the oven and let it rest for about 15 minutes. Raise the oven heat to 450°F (230°C, or gas mark 8). Spoon the snowcap mixture on top of the cake. Return the cake to the oven (not in the bain-marie). Bake for 10 minutes. Remove the cake from the oven and let cool in the pan. When the cake comes to room temperature, refrigerate it until thoroughly cold.

Yield: Makes 12 servings

DID YOU KNOW? Cheesecake is the traditional, go-to dish for the Jewish holiday of Shavuot.

ACKNOWLEDGMENTS

I could not have gone forward with this book without the help of my agent, Marilyn Allen at Allen O'Shea Literary Agency, and Jessica Haberman, acquiring editor at Fair Winds Press, both of whom not only believed in this project but whose energy and enthusiasm kept me going through the deadlines. I am very grateful to my tasters: my husband Ed and children Meredith and Greg, Gillian, and Jesse; and to Eileen and Jeff, Leslie and Neil, Susan and Richard, Robbie and Connie, all of whom dined, nibbled, and noshed and gave their honest critiques. Thanks to my grandchildren Zev, Lila, Nina, Remy, and Carina, loves of my life, and to whom this book is dedicated, just for being. Of course I must acknowledge the fine, detailed, and dedicated work of Cara Connors, project manager; Kathy Dragolich, copyeditor; Glenn Scott, who took the beautiful photographs of the food; Katie Fawkes, marketing manager; and all the other folks on the Fair Winds team who made this book possible: thanks to you all.

ABOUT THE AUTHOR

Ronnie Fein is a long-time food writer. She currently writes regular features for the food sections of *The Connecticut Post, Stamford Advocate*, and *Greenwich Time*, and writes online for *The Jewish Week, Joy of Kosher, Koshereye*, and others. She also writes for the *New Jewish Voice, Connecticut Bride, Connecticut Magazine*, and *Jewish Woman Magazine*. She has her own food blog, *Kitchen Vignettes*, at www.ronniefein.com.

Ronnie has authored three cookbooks, *The Complete Idiot's Guide to Cooking Basics, The Complete Idiot's Guide to American Cooking*, and *Hip Kosher*. She was also a contributing editor to *The New Cook's Catalogue*.

Ronnie operates the Ronnie Fein School of Creative Cooking in Stamford, Connecticut, where she lives with her husband. She has two married daughters and five grandchildren.

INDEX